UNDERSTANDING
English
Pronunciation

An integrated practice course

Susan Boyer

Boyer Educational Resources 2001
Reprinted 2004, 2006, 2007, 2008, 2012, 2022

Boyer Educational Resources
PO Box 255, Glenbrook 2773
e-mail: info@boyereducation.com.au

Acknowledgments:

I would like to express my thanks to the following people for their contribution to the final presentation of this book:

Firstly, I would like to thank all the teachers who trialled material contained in this book and suggested improvements. I am grateful also to my colleagues who have provided constructive feedback at various stages in the development of this book. In particular I would like to thank Dr Ruth Nichols, Sheila Addison, Alison Hey, Dr Helen Fraser, Ross Forman, Tanya Roddan, Peter Richards, Veronica Dickson, Susan Perry, James Knight, Nadia Whitehead, Polly Wells and Peter Goldworthy for their valued comments. I would like to say thank you to Darrell Hilton for the production of the accompanying audio recording and to Jeanette Christian for her careful proofreading. And of course, I am particularly indebted to the many students who have given me the necessary insight into the pronunciation needs of English language learners.

Also, I want to thank my husband Len for his encouragement and support throughout the project, as well as the many hours he spent in the production of this resource.

Illustrations on pages 46, 53, 56, 66, 82, and 116 are by Matthew J Larwood.

Images used herein were obtained from IMSI's MasterClips Collection,
1895 Francisco Blvd. East, San Rafael, CA 94901-5506, USA

National Library of Australia
Cataloguing-in-Publication data:

Boyer, Susan
Understanding English Pronunciation: an integrated practice course.
ISBN 978-0-9585395-7-9

1) English language - Australia - Pronunciation
2) English language - Spoken English - Australia
   Textbook for foreign speakers

421.52

Printed by: Lightning Source, Vic, Australia

© Boyer Educational Resources:
   e-mail: info@boyereducation.com.au
   www.boyereducation.com.au
   www.englishebooks.com.au (for download of eBook (PDF) & eAudio (MP3) versions of our resources)

ABOUT THIS BOOK

Understanding English Pronunciation - an integrated practice course has been designed so students can work through it in class with other students, or alone, without the help of a teacher. Each unit of the course is based on a different topic and focuses on different sounds and features of English pronunciation.

Each unit is divided into different parts which introduce and practise various aspects of pronunciation in a systematic and enjoyable way, while also providing interesting topics through which to practise pronunciation.

Unit 1 provides an introduction to English pronunciation, using a dictionary, and a listening test.

Units 2 – 12 contain the following sections:

Preliminary Listening introduces the particular vowel sounds in focus for the unit.

Part 1 - Introduction to the topic

Part 1 introduces the topic and vocabulary needed to analyse the particular sounds in focus.
In Part 1A you will listen to the text, focus on the meaning and become familiar with the vocabulary.

Part 2 - Focus on Pronunciation

In Part 2 you will analyse the sounds featured in the text in Part 1, as well as additional features of English pronunciation.

Part 3 - Extending the topic

This section introduces more vocabulary which contain the sounds in focus as well as extending the topic.

Part 4 - Analysing the sounds

This section focuses on sound discrimination and helps you to 'tune your ears' to particular sounds of English.

Part 5 - Understanding the link between spoken and written English

You will analyse ways of spelling the sounds in focus and see some patterns to English spelling.

Part 6 - Spelling Check - Dictation

Now it's time to test yourself and see what you have learnt by trying the spelling check.
You are asked to complete the text as you listen again to the text that was introduced in Part 1.

Part 7 - Further Listening and Speaking Practice

This section provides more valuable listening and speaking practice as you:
a) listen to and practise questions or conversation relating to the topic of the unit.
b) distinguish between, and practise pronouncing the featured sounds fluently so that you are understood by other people.
c) practise features of English pronunciation such as stress and intonation, along with fluency.

Part 8 and 9 - Review or extension activity

These sections summarise or extend the topic through informative activities, while providing further pronunciation practice of the featured sounds. In some units, additional sounds are practised.

Dear Student of English

Welcome to *Understanding English Pronunciation - an integrated practice course.*
This book, along with its associated audio recording, has been designed to help you to understand English pronunciation and to speak English more clearly and fluently.

As you listen to the audio recording you will hear the speakers give models of the pronunciation of individual words, as well as words within sentences and conversations.

Important note to students about pronunciation

- It is important to realise that the pronunciation of a sound can change, depending on the other sounds around it in a word and that the pronunciation of words can change depending on how they are used in a sentence. The pronunciation of a word spoken slowly or singly may be different from the pronunciation of the same word spoken within the context of natural conversation. This principle applies to most languages – not only English.

- It is important to realise that no two people (even speakers of the same language) pronounce sounds and words *exactly* the same way. That's why you can recognise someone you know by their voice even when you can't see them!

  Look at the examples of the word *pronunciation* written in different handwriting below.
  The letters are written differently but you can see they form the same word.

pronunciation   pronunciation   **pronunciation**   *pronunciation*   pronunciation

It is similar with spoken language. Though different speakers of the same language may pronounce words with slightly different pronunciation, listeners need to be able to recognise and understand which words are being spoken. For example, you will notice that the speakers on the audio recording pronounce the words *'answer'* and *'example'* a little differently from each other. However, as the words are easily understood by all speakers of English, the variation in pronunciation does not cause communication problems.

The important thing to remember when learning a new language is that your pronunciation needs to be intelligible. This means that you can be understood without difficulty. The aim of this course is to build your confidence when listening to speakers of English and help you to improve your pronunciation of English.

I hope you enjoy and benefit from using *Understanding English Pronunciation.*

Susan Boyer

Suggestions for students working through this course independently:

➢ Practise speaking English every day. Try to use the new words you have learnt.

➢ Write new or difficult words onto small cards or a small notebook that you can carry in your pocket or wallet. Remember to check the stress patterns and mark the words so that you can practise the correct pronunciation.

➢ Listen to English speakers every day. Ask the meaning and pronunciation of unfamiliar words.

➢ When listening to speakers of English, notice the way words are linked; notice how intonation is used to convey meaning and notice how speakers pause to focus on important information.

➢ When using this book with the audio recording, practise saying the new words aloud. Record your voice so that you can check your pronunciation.

➢ After listening several times to the recorded sentences in Part 7 (Units 2 – 12), practise reading the sentences aloud. Record your voice so that you can check your pronunciation.

➢ As you listen to your voice (on the recording), write the sentences you hear. Then compare your written sentences with the sentences in the book. Do you <u>say the same words</u> as the speaker on the recording?

➢ Compare <u>your</u> pronunciation with the <u>speaker</u> on the *Understanding English Pronunciation* recording. Do you <u>stress the same words</u>? Do you <u>use the same intonation</u>?

Symbols for instruction used in this book:

means listen to the audio recording

means do the written exercise

means discuss or practise

You will need to check words in a dictionary, so have a good dictionary nearby while you are studying. Because English words are not always pronounced as they are spelt, you will also need to use a dictionary to learn the correct pronunciation. A <u>good</u> dictionary will give you clear examples of pronunciation and a Pronunciation Key.

Glossary of pronunciation terms

Use this list as a reference as you are using this book:

vowel letters	There are _five_ vowel _letters_ in the English alphabet. These are: **a, e, i, o, u.**
vowel sounds and symbols	There are _twelve_ vowel _sounds_ in English represented by phonemic **symbols**. There are seven short sounds: /æ/, /e/, /ə/, /ʊ/, /ʌ /, /ɪ/, /ɒ/ * as well as five longer sounds, /ɑ:/, /i:/, /ɔ:/, /ɜ:/, /u:/ - a long sound is often indicated by **:** *Note: Some varieties of North American English do not use the vowel sound /ɒ/ as in the word '_hot_'; The short sound /ɒ/ is replaced by the longer sound /ɑ:/ making '_hot'_ sound like '_heart'_.
schwa	The most frequently used of all English vowel sounds, is the **un**stressed sound /ə/. The sound and symbol /ə/ are called '**schwa'**.
diphthongs	Diphthong sounds are made from two vowel sounds put together. There are eight diphthongs: /eɪ/, /aɪ/, /ɔɪ/, /eə/, /ɪə/, /ʊə/, /aʊ/ and /əʊ/ (also shown as /oʊ/ For examples of words containing these sounds see the Phonemic Chart (p. 154)
consonant letters	Letters in the English alphabet which are not vowels are called consonants. These are: **b, c, d, f, g, h, j, k, l, m, n, p, q, r, s, t, v, w, x, y, z.**
consonant sounds	Additional _consonant sounds_ (represented by the following symbols) are: /θ/, /ð/, /ʃ/, /tʃ/, / ʒ /, /dʒ /, /ŋ/. Check the phonemic chart (p. 154) for examples.
syllable	Spoken words are formed with **syllables**, meaning **units of sound**. A syllable is a unit of unbroken sound, usually containing a vowel sound.
contraction	When two words are contracted (shortened) and linked together they form a contraction. The missing letters are shown with an apostrophe ('). For example, I have = I've; we would = we'd; he will = he'll.
word stress	Words with more than one syllable, one syllable is usually stronger (spoken more clearly) than the other(s). The term _stressed_ syllable refers to the strongest (primary) syllable in words of more than one syllable. eg. '**tra**vel
utterance	An utterance is a spoken message. It can be a complete sentence or one or two words. eg 'Oh no!' 'When?'
stress within utterances	In spoken English, words which carry the main message of the sentence contain _stressed_ syllables. Stressing the important words helps the listener to hear the message of the speaker. eg. I _want_ to go _home_.
prominent words	These are the words that the speaker makes _most_ prominent in an utterance. They signal the most important piece of information. They are also called **focus words**. See Unit 4, Part 7 for an explanation and examples.
connected speech	When native speakers of English talk with natural conversational speed, they use _connected_ speech. This means they speak **fluently**. Their words are not spoken separately but are **linked** together, without stopping after each word.
intonation	Intonation refers to the rising and falling tones in our voice, which in English, are used to express meaning. See Unit 5, Part 7 for some general patterns.

Understanding English Pronunciation - Contents

About this book
Important notes for students
Glossary of Pronunciation Terms

Unit 1
Introduction to English Pronunciation

- What is pronunciation?

- What makes the many languages of the world different?

- Which sounds of English are different to those of your first language?

- In your language, how is important information highlighted when speaking?

- Which aspects of English pronunciation do you find most difficult?

In Unit 1 you will learn

- how dictionaries can help with the pronunciation of English words
- the importance of 'stress' in the pronunciation of English.

Part 1 - The Sounds of English

Listen as you read the information.

The Sounds of English

There are twenty six *letters* in the English alphabet, including five vowel letters, **a, e, i, o, u**, and twenty one consonant letters, **b, c, d, f, g, h, j, k, l, m, n, p, q, r, s, t, v, w, x, y, z**.

There are, however, *over forty sounds used to speak English.*

Because there are *more sounds in spoken English than there are letters in written English,* dictionaries and pronunciation text books use *symbols to represent each of the different sounds.*

It is *not necessary to memorise* all the sound symbols of English, however it is *very helpful* to understand how your dictionary uses symbols to represent English sounds.

A Pronunciation Guide (or Pronunciation Key) will usually be within the first few pages of your dictionary (or in the front or back cover).

- **Stop the audio recording and find the pronunciation guide in your dictionary now.**

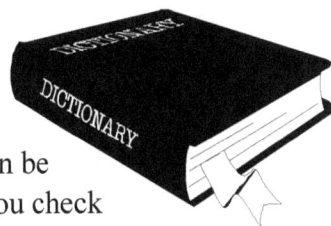

Read the following information:

Because English words are not always pronounced as they are spelt, it can be helpful to use your dictionary to learn the correct pronunciation. When you check a word in your dictionary, the pronunciation may be shown with the sound symbols between two lines / /. For example, the pronunciation of the word *six* may be shown as /sɪks/.

Many dictionaries use the same pronunciation symbols as those used in this book. The symbols used in this book are based on the **International Phonetic Alphabet**. A complete chart of English sound symbols (called phonemic symbols) is displayed on page 154 of this book, with example words to explain each sound.

Exercise 1A - Review

1) How many <u>letters</u> are there in written English?   _____

2) How many <u>sounds</u> are used in spoken English?   _____

3) What do dictionaries and pronunciation text books
   use to explain the sounds of English letters and words?   _____

Using a Dictionary Pronunciation Guide

A <u>useful</u> dictionary will have a pronunciation guide and give clear examples of pronunciation.

Many dictionaries use the same pronunciation symbols as the *Phonemic Chart* shown in the back of this book. However, some dictionaries use different symbols, so to avoid confusion it's important to check which symbols *your* dictionary uses.

For example, some dictionaries show the long vowel sound in the word *'see'* as /si:/
Some dictionaries use line on top of the vowel to show the same sound in *'see'* as /sē/

Exercise 1B - Dictionary Practice

1)
- Using *your* dictionary, find the word *'sit'* and the word *'seat'*.
- Notice the symbol used to show the <u>vowel sound</u> in *'sit'*, and the <u>vowel sound</u> in *'seat'*.
- Copy the symbols from your dictionary onto the lines below.

Your dictionary symbols   Your dictionary symbols

short vowel sound in s<u>i</u>t = _____   **long** vowel sound in s<u>ea</u>t = _____

2)
- Using *your dictionary,* find the word *'hard'* and the word *'heart'*.
- Notice the symbol used to show the <u>vowel sound</u> in '*h<u>ar</u>d*' and the vowel sound in '*h<u>ea</u>rt*'
  are the same (though the spelling is different).
- Copy the symbols from your dictionary onto the lines below.

Your dictionary symbols   Your dictionary symbols

long vowel sound in h<u>ar</u>d = _____   **long** vowel sound in h<u>ea</u>rt = _____

Part 2 – The importance of 'stress' in English pronunciation

As well as understanding and recognising the different sounds of English, it's important to understand how *stress* is used in English to show meaning.

In English, some parts of words are spoken more strongly or loudly than others. This is called *word stress*. The meaning of a word may be affected by the way the word is stressed.

Look at the following words as examples: 1) present (gift), 2) present (give, show)
Now listen to the way the words are stressed differently in the following listening exercise:

🎧 **Exercise 2A** **Listen:**

In example 1, the first part of the word is stressed: **present**

In example 2, the second part of the word is stressed: **present**

Using Your Dictionary

A good dictionary will provide very useful information on how to stress words correctly.

In your dictionary, near the *Pronunciation Key*, you should find an explanation of how *word stress* is shown on all words listed in the dictionary. Find this in your dictionary now.

Dictionaries use various ways to show which part of a word should be *stressed*.
For example, in the word *present* (meaning *gift*), the stress is on the first part of the word.

The following examples show how word stress may be shown in a dictionary.

- some dictionaries show a small stress mark ' *above* the stressed part of the word.   eg. présənt
- some dictionaries show a small stress mark ' *before and above* the stressed part.   eg. ˈpre sənt
- some dictionaries show a small stress mark ' *after and above* the stressed part.   eg. presˈənt
- some dictionaries use *a line under* the stressed part, to show the stressed syllable. eg. presənt

To avoid confusion, check how *your* dictionary shows word stress.

Exercise 2B Check the word '*present*' *(gift)* in your dictionary. How is the stress shown?

Stress within utterances

As well as understanding how stress is used in words, it's important to understand how stress is used within *utterances*. An utterance is a spoken message. It can be a complete sentence or one or two words. eg *'Oh no!'* In English, speakers stress the words which give information.

🎧 **Exercise 2C** **Listen**: Can you hear the way the speaker stresses only the important words?

(Stress is used in the underlined words.)

*'She was **pleased** with the **present**.'*

In order to speak any language correctly, it's necessary to hear and distinguish the sounds of the language correctly. How we *hear* sounds is related to the way we *pronounce* sounds.
Try this test! Check your answers when you have finished all *Listening Exercises* (1 – 4).

Listening Test - Exercise 1

🦻 **Listen and tick ☑ the sentence (a) or (b), that you hear.**

(The first one has been done as an example.)

1) ☐ a) They're <u>living</u> on a boat.
   ☑ b) They're <u>leaving</u> on a boat.

2) ☐ a) I left my <u>cap</u> in the kitchen.
   ☐ b) I left my <u>cup</u> in the kitchen.

3) ☐ a) Have they <u>packed</u> the car yet?
   ☐ b) Have they <u>parked</u> the car yet?

4) ☐ a) How do you spell '<u>full</u>'?
   ☐ b) How do you spell '<u>fool</u>'?

5) ☐ a) I need a <u>desk</u> for my computer.
   ☐ b) I need a <u>disk</u> for my computer.

6) ☐ a) Did you see the little boy's <u>mouth</u>?
   ☐ b) Did you see the little boy's <u>mouse</u>?

7) ☐ a) How many <u>pairs</u> did you see?
   ☐ b) How many <u>bears</u> did you see?

8) ☐ a) Where's the <u>pen</u>?
   ☐ b) Where's the <u>pain</u>?

9) ☐ a) I <u>worked</u> for a long time today.
   ☐ b) I <u>walked</u> for a long time today.

10) ☐ a) Did he finish his <u>rice</u>?
    ☐ b) Did he finish his <u>race</u>?

11) ☐ a) They <u>want</u> work.
    ☐ b) They <u>won't</u> work.

12) ☐ a) They went the <u>long</u> way.
    ☐ b) They went the <u>wrong</u> way.

13) ☐ a) The <u>men</u> listened to the story.
    ☐ b) The <u>man</u> listened to the story.

Listening Test - Exercise 2

In English, word stress helps the listener to recognise words correctly.
The following words are spelt the same but are stressed differently, producing different meanings.

🦻 **Listen and tick ☑ the word (a) or (b) that you hear. (The stressed part is <u>underlined</u>.)**

1) ☐ a) <u>pre</u>sent
   ☐ b) pre<u>sent</u>

2) ☐ a) <u>ob</u>ject
   ☐ b) ob<u>ject</u>

3) ☐ a) <u>de</u>sert
   ☐ b) de<u>sert</u>

4) ☐ a) <u>pro</u>duce
   ☐ b) pro<u>duce</u>

Listening Test - Exercise 3

In English conversation, speakers stress some words more strongly than others. The stressed words help the listener to focus on the important information in the utterance.

Listen and <u>underline</u> the words that are stressed by the speakers.

(The first line has been done as an example. If necessary, pause the recording after each line.)

A: Could you <u>tell</u> me where the <u>bank</u> is <u>please</u>?

B: Yes, in High Street, on the left, near the library.

A: Thanks. And is there somewhere to park the car?

B: There's a place just next to the bank but you'll have to pay.

A: Oh. Do you know what they charge?

B: I don't, I'm sorry - but there'll be a sign at the gate with the price.

         There's also a place near the station. It's usually full but you could check.

A: OK. Thanks for your help.

Listening Test – Exercise 4

When spoken at natural conversational speed, English words are not always heard distinctly, but are often linked together.

Listen and write what the speakers say.

Pause the recording after each line you write the sentence.

1) _____

2) _____

3) _____

4) _____

5) _____

Check your answers on page 128 before continuing.

Check your answers on page 128 before continuing.

The exercises throughout this book will help you practise and improve your listening, speaking and understanding of English.

There is a Progress Check after Unit 5.

Unit 2
Language Study

1) Why can learning a new language be a challenge?

2) What is needed for successful language study?

3) What does it mean to be 'an active learner'?

In this unit you will:

- Discuss the topic of Language Study

- Practise distinguishing between the sounds /æ/ (as in *fan*) and /ʌ/ (as in *fun*)

- Practise pronouncing the sounds /æ/ and /ʌ/ in fluent speech

- Analyse the link between spoken and written English ie. ways of spelling the sounds /æ/ and /ʌ/

- Learn about syllables in words

Preliminary Listening

Listen to the vowel sounds in the following words. Can you hear the difference?

/æ/ fan	/æ/ ankle	/æ/ cap	/æ/ match
/ʌ/ fun	/ʌ/ uncle	/ʌ/ cup	/ʌ/ much

Note: The sound /æ/ as in the word 'fan', and /ʌ/ as in 'fun', may be represented with different symbols in your dictionary, so check the words in <u>your</u> dictionary now. What symbols does your dictionary use?

Part 1 - Introduction to the topic

Think about the topic before turning the page to read and listen to the text.

The speaker will talk about *Language Study*. What do you think the speaker will say?

☐ a) When studying a new language it's important not to make mistakes.

or

☐ b) When learning a new language, it's important to remember that making mistakes is a natural part of learning.

Check your answer by listening to Part 1A.

In Part 1, focus on *what* the speaker says about the topic.
You will focus on *how* words are pronounced in Part 2.

1A Listen as you read the text about *Language Study*.

Note: The text is spoken more slowly than natural conversational speech.

Language Study

Studying a new language can be a <u>challenge</u>. Some language learners worry very much if listeners have <u>trouble</u> understanding their <u>accent</u> or when people <u>mutter</u> expressions they don't understand. But with a plan of action and regular practice, most people can reach a good <u>standard</u> of communication in a second language. Pronunciation practice is an important <u>matter</u> when studying a new language, as incorrect pronunciation can cause misunderstandings. The plan of most adult language learners however, isn't to <u>match</u> the pronunciation of native speakers but to have <u>comfortable</u> communication in everyday business and social situations.

When studying a new language, it's important to remember that making mistakes is a natural part of learning. Being an active, rather than a <u>passive</u> learner means using every opportunity to practise your language skills, so be prepared to ask for help and correction. Most people are happy to help learners with the pronunciation or meaning of an <u>unfamiliar</u> word. Studying a new language can be a challenge but it can also be a wonderful way of meeting new friends and learning about other cultures.

1B Write the underlined words in the text next to the correct meaning below.
The first one has been done as an example.

1) difficult & new experience   *challenge*   6) level/grade   _____

2) way of pronunciation   _____   7) subject/situation   _____

3) speak <u>un</u>clearly, quietly   _____   8) not active   _____

4) be the same as   _____   9) problems   _____

5) easy/ with no trouble   _____   10) unknown/new   _____

1B Listen and check your answers to 1B. Repeat the words after the speaker.

1C Now discuss the following questions:

1) Why can learning a new language be a challenge?

2) What is needed for successful language study?

3) What does it mean to be 'an active learner'?

Part 2 - Focus on Pronunciation

👂 **2A** **Listen to the underlined vowel sound in the following words.**

Which words contain the sound /æ/ as in *fan*? Which words contain the sound /ʌ/ as in *fun*?

s<u>o</u>me	w<u>o</u>rry	ch<u>a</u>llenge	m<u>u</u>ch	tr<u>ou</u>ble	<u>a</u>ccent	m<u>u</u>tter
st<u>a</u>ndard	m<u>a</u>tter	pl<u>a</u>n	pr<u>a</u>ctise	m<u>a</u>tch	<u>a</u>ctive	<u>o</u>ther	c<u>u</u>ltures

◄◄ **Replay the recording of 2A. Pause the recording after each word.**
Write the words in the correct lists below, according to the underlined sound.
Don't be confused by the *spelling*. You need to listen to the *pronunciation* of the words!

1) Sound /æ/ as in the word *fan*	2) Sound /ʌ/ as in the word *fun*
	s<u>o</u>me

Check your answers on page 129 before continuing.

Syllables in words

Spoken words are formed with *syllables*. A syllable is formed when individual sounds are pronounced together to make one unit of unbroken sound within a word.

👂 **2B** **Listen to the following examples:**

Words with one syllable	Words with two syllables
match some plan have	*active study language passive*

In order to pronounce an English word correctly, you need to know how many syllables it contains.

👂 **2C** **Listen and decide how many syllables each word contains.**
Write the number of syllables. Two have been done as examples.

some	1	worry	2	challenge	☐
much	☐	trouble	☐	accent	☐
mutter	☐	standard	☐	matter	☐
plan	☐	practise	☐	match	☐
active	☐	other	☐	cultures	☐

- Syllables will also be practised further in Unit 3.

Part 3 - Extending the topic

In Part 3, focus on *what* the speaker says about the topic.
You will focus on *how* words are pronounced in Part 4.

🦻 **3A   Listen to the extended text on *Language Study*.**

Language Study

Studying a new language can be a challenge. Some language learners worry very much if listeners have trouble understanding their accent or when people mutter expressions they don't understand. But with a plan of action and regular practice, most people can reach a good standard of communication in a second language. Pronunciation practice is an important matter when studying a new language, as incorrect pronunciation can cause misunderstandings. The plan of most adult language learners however, isn't to match the pronunciation of native speakers but to have comfortable communication in everyday business and social situations.

When studying a new language, it's important to remember that making mistakes is a natural part of learning. Being an active, rather than a passive learner means using every opportunity to practise your language skills, so be prepared to ask for help and correction. Most people are happy to help learners with the pronunciation or meaning of an unfamiliar word. Studying a new language can be a challenge but it can also be a wonderful way of meeting new friends and learning about other cultures.

Just as an actor or actress needs to study and practise a new accent in order to act in a natural way, so you too as a language learner, must become a language analyst. As well as learning new words and grammar, you must adapt to a new category of sounds. As an adult learner you'll also need to practise new ways of moving your tongue and understand how small changes in your voice can change the meaning. It's also important to be aware of the relationship between English spelling and pronunciation.

Success in language learning isn't a matter of luck; you need lots of practice. Lack of practice is the main reason for lack of progress. Of course, don't expect results in a hurry; learning a language takes more than a couple of months. Having access to the right equipment will encourage you to practise. You'll need a dictionary that gives clear examples of pronunciation and access to audio equipment so you can record your speech and check your improvement. It's also important to have a positive attitude to the experience of language study.

3B - Extending your vocabulary

✏️   **Find and underline the following words in the last two paragraphs of the text above.**

analyst	adapt	category	tongue	attitude	lack
luck	(in a) hurry	encourage	access (to)	results	

Unit 2 – Language Study

Match the words you have underlined in the text with the correct meaning listed below. One has been done as an example.

1) have the use of (something)	_access (to)_	6) fortune	_____
2) person who examines in detail	_____	7) group, set	_____
3) main organ of speech	_____	8) way of thinking	_____
4) become used to new conditions	_____	9) assist, help	_____
5) absence, be without	_____	10) the end product	_____
		11) quickly (in a short time)	_____

3B Listen and check your answers to 3B. Repeat the words after the speaker.

Part 4 - Analysing the sounds

◀◀ **Replay 3B and listen to the pronunciation of the stressed syllable in each word.**
(If necessary, pause the recording after each word.)

Write the words in the correct columns below, then check your answers on page 129.

1) Words with the sound /æ/ (as in _fan_)	2) Words with the sound /ʌ/ (as in _fun_)
access _analyst_	

Part 5 - Understanding the link between spoken and written English

Spelling Lists - Ways of _spelling the sound_ /æ/ (as in the word _fan_)

The sound /æ/ is almost always spelt with the letter 'a'. Look at the following examples.

a̱ccent	a̱ctive	ma̱tch	pla̱n	pra̱ctice	language

Spelling Lists - Ways of _spelling the sound_ /ʌ/ (as in the word _fun_)

u	o	ou
mu̱ch	so̱me	trou̱ble
u̱nderstand	co̱me	cou̱ntry
cu̱lture	mo̱ney	you̱ng

Part 6 - Spelling Check – Dictation

👂 Listen to the *Language Study* text again.

✏️ Complete the text with the correct words. (Pause the recording to write the words.)

Language Study

Studying a new language can be a _____. Some language learners _____ very _____ if listeners have _____understanding their _____or when people _____ expressions they don't understand. But with a plan of action and regular practice, most people can reach a good _____of communication in a second language. Pronunciation practice is an important _____when studying a new language, as incorrect pronunciation can cause misunderstandings. The _____ of most _____ language learners however, isn't to _____the pronunciation of native speakers but to have comfortable communication in everyday business and social situations.

When studying a new language, it's important to remember that making mistakes is a natural part of learning. Being an _____, rather than a _____ learner means using every opportunity to practise your language skills; so be prepared to ask for help and correction. Most people are _____ to help learners with the pronunciation or meaning of an unfamiliar word. Studying a new language can be a _____ but it can also be a _____ way of meeting new friends and learning about _____ cultures.

Check your answers by comparing this page with the *Language Study* text – Part 1A.

Part 7 - Listening Practice

In natural English speech, words are not always spoken distinctly but are linked together. You are going to listen to someone asking questions about language study.

👂 **7A** Listen and complete the questions. (Pause the recording after each line.)
✏️ Write the words you hear.

1) _____ when people don't understand your accent?

2) _____ practise a new language?

3) _____ dictionary to check pronunciation?

4) _____ successful in language study?

Did you notice that some words are easier to hear than others? You will learn about this in Unit 3.

Check your answers on page 129 before continuing.

Distinguishing between the sounds /æ/ and /ʌ/ in fluent speech

Underline the words which are different in sentences a) and b) below. The first one has been done as an example.

7B   **Listen and tick ☑ the sentence, a) or b) that you hear.**

1) ☐ a) The <u>fan</u> was shared by everyone.
    ☐ b) The <u>fun</u> was shared by everyone.

2) ☐ a) How's your ankle?
    ☐ b) How's your uncle?

3) ☐ a) Did you see the track near the side of the road? (path for walking)
    ☐ b) Did you see the truck near the side of the road?

4) ☐ a) They don't matter much, so don't worry. (matter = to be important)
    ☐ b) They don't mutter much, so don't worry. (mutter = to speak unclearly)

5) ☐ a) She likes clothes to match. (to match = be compatible/fit together)
    ☐ b) She likes clothes too much.

6) ☐ a) The sick old man mattered to the kind doctor. (mattered = was important)
    ☐ b) The sick old man muttered to the kind doctor. (muttered = spoke unclearly)

7) ☐ a) Where could I buy a new cap?
    ☐ b) Where could I buy a new cup?

8) ☐ a) They found a hat in the forest.
    ☐ b) They found a hut in the forest.   (hut = very small, simple house)

Check your answers on page 130 before continuing.

Now practise pronouncing the sentences correctly. Work with a partner.

- One person should say sentence a) or b).

- The other person should decide which sentence he/she hears.

Part 8 – Contractions

In spoken English, some words may be difficult to hear because they are linked to other words. Some linked words are called 'contractions'. For example, instead of saying, *I am...* speakers say *I'm...* The linked words are often pronounced as one syllable but not always.

8A Listen to the way the pronunciation of words changes when they are contracted. Write the number of syllables you hear when the words are contracted.

Full form	Contraction	How many syllables?
I am........................	I'm	1
He is........................	He's	
She is.......................	She's	
It is..........................	It's	
There is.....................	There's	
You are......................	You're	
We are...	We're /weə/	
They are....................	They're /ðeə/	
I would (also *had*)	I'd	
He would....................	He'd	
They would.................	They'd	
It Would....................	It'd	
I will........................	I'll	
You will.....................	You'll	
It will	It'll	
I have.......................	I've	
You have...................	You've	
We have....................	We've	
They have.................	They've	
Full form	**Negative contractions**	
is not........................	isn't	
are not	aren't	
were not	weren't	
can not.....................	can't	
could not...................	couldn't	
do not.......................	don't	
will not......................	won't	

Notice the correct position for the apostrophe (') when contractions are written.

8B

a) How many times does the speaker use a contraction in Part 3A, *Language Study* text?
b) Which are pronounced as one syllable? Which are pronounced as two syllables?

Check your answers on page 130 before continuing.

Part 9 - Syllables and Word Stress

Syllables - Review

- Spoken words are formed with syllables (or units of sound).

- A syllable is formed when individual sounds are pronounced together to form one unit of unbroken sound within a word.

- A word may contain one or more syllables.

For example: 'come' = one syllable; 'welcome' = two syllables; 'unwelcome' = three syllables

Word Stress - Pronouncing syllables correctly

In English words, some syllables are naturally pronounced more clearly or strongly than others.

- The strong syllables are known as *stressed* syllables.
- The weak syllables are known as *unstressed* syllables.

In the following words, the first syllable is stronger than the second syllable.

<u>cha</u>llenge
<u>cul</u>ture   The **stressed** (strong) syllables are underlined.
<u>se</u>cond

In the following words, the second syllable is stronger.

a<u>**bove**</u>
pro<u>**nounce**</u>
a<u>**part**</u>

Using stress correctly is a *very* important part of English pronunciation.
In most dictionaries, unstressed syllables in words are shown by the symbol /ə/.

Most dictionaries show stress in words with the mark ' (before or after the stressed syllable).
For example, in the Oxford Dictionary the pronunciation of 'second' is represented as /se'kənd/.

In Unit 3 you will analyse the unstressed sound /ə/. It is the most common sound in English.
Understanding the sound /ə/ will help you to use stress correctly in English words.

Unit 3
Other Cultures

- How much do you know about other cultures?

- How important is it to know about the cultures of the people you meet socially and for business?

In this unit you will:

- Discuss the topic of *Other Cultures*.

- Practise identifying strong and weak syllables in words.

- Practise using the unstressed, weak sound /ə/.

- Understand the importance of 'stress' in English pronunciation.

- Analyse the link between spoken and written English
  ie. ways of spelling the sound /ə/.

- Practise pronouncing the letter combination 'th' correctly.

English pronunciation consists of *stressed* (strong) and *unstressed* (weak) sounds.
The symbol /ə/ is used in most dictionaries to represent the *unstressed sound* in words.

Preliminary Listening

Listen to the following pairs of words.

Each pair has the same spelling but the <u>stress</u>, or stronger sound, is in a different place.
The different stress pattern changes the meaning. (The stressed syllable is <u>underlined</u>.)

present	**de**sert	**in**valid
pre**sent**	de**sert**	in**val**id

In this unit you will study the importance of correct stress patterns in English.

Part 1 - Introduction to the topic

Think about the topic before turning the page to read and listen to the text.

What do you think the speaker will say about *Other Cultures*?

☐ a) Many people think that learning about other cultures is unimportant.

or

☐ b) Many people think that learning about other cultures is educational and rewarding.

Check your answer by listening to 1A.

In Part 1, focus on *what* the speaker says about the topic.
You will focus on *how* words are pronounced in Part 2.

👂 1A   Listen as you read the text about *Other Cultures*.

Other Cultures

What is culture? Culture means the way of living of a particular
group of people. People from different cultures grow up with different
customs, beliefs and <u>values</u>. For example, if you travel from one country
to another, you'll probably find the people do some things very differently
to the ways you are <u>familiar with</u> in your culture. Culture is usually passed
from parents to children for many <u>generations,</u> so people sometimes believe
that their culture is the only correct way to live.

Do you think everyone in the world should do things as you do them in your culture or
are you <u>open-minded</u> about other customs? Many people believe that learning about
other cultures can be <u>educational</u> and <u>rewarding</u>.

✏️ 1B Write the underlined words in the text next to the correct meaning below.
The first one has been done as an example.

1) standards/ideas about what
   is important   *values*

2) useful for learning   _____

3) willing to accept new ideas   _____

4) satisfying,
   worthwhile   _____

5) know well   _____

6) life times   _____

👂 1B   Listen and check your answers to 1B. Repeat the words after the speaker.

Notice that some syllables are pronounced more strongly than other syllables.

👥 1C - Now discuss the following questions.

What is meant by the word 'culture'?

Why do some people believe their culture is the only correct way to live?

Part 2 - Focus on pronunciation - introduction to the unstressed sound /ə/

- **Read this information before doing the following exercises.**

English pronunciation consists of *stressed* and *unstressed* syllables.
Using stressed and unstressed sounds correctly is an important part of English pronunciation.

The unstressed sound is represented in the dictionary with the symbol /ə/.
The sound /ə/, which is called *schwa*, is <u>the most commonly used sound in English.</u>

2A **Listen to the following words. Each word has two syllables.**

The *second* syllable is an unstressed, weak sound.

/ə/
travel

/ə/
welcome

/ə/
people

stressed (strong) syllables are **underlined**
/ə/ shows *unstressed* (weak) syllable

Listen to the following words. The *first* syllable is an unstressed, weak sound.

/ə/
be**liefs**

/ə/
a**bout**

/ə/
co**rrect**

Dictionary practice:
Check the words in Exercise 2A in your dictionary.
The symbol /ə/ is used in most dictionaries to indicate *un*stressed syllables in words.
Which symbol does your dictionary use?

2B **Listen to the following two-syllable words.**

Write the schwa symbol /ə/ above the *un*stressed syllable, as in the example.
Underline the stressed (strong) syllable.

/ə/						
people	*problem*	*collect*	*listen*	*pattern*	*along*	*second*

2C - Check the words above in your dictionary.
The *unstressed* syllable will likely be shown with the symbol /ə/.
Did you hear the unstressed sound in the correct place?
If not, listen again.

Using your Dictionary – Review

A good dictionary will provide very useful information on how to pronounce words correctly.

As well as using the symbol /ə/ to indicate **unstressed** syllables, dictionaries use various ways to show which syllable should be **stressed**.

For example, in the word *festival* (which has three syllables), the stress is on the first syllable The second and third syllables are unstressed. Look how this may be shown in a dictionary.

* some dictionaries show a small stress mark ' *before and above* the stressed syllable. eg. ′fes təvəl
* some dictionaries show a small stress mark ' *after and above* the stressed syllable.   eg. fes′təvəl
* some dictionaries use *a line under* the stressed sound, to show the stressed syllable. eg. fes̲təvəl

To avoid confusion, always check which stress symbol *your* dictionary uses.

Check the word *festival* in your dictionary. How is the *stressed* syllable shown?

Now let's analyse how stressed and unstressed syllables are used in spoken language to create the rhythm of English.

Now you will learn how stress is used within utterances. An *utterance* is a spoken message.

It can be a complete sentence or it can be one or two words.

👂 **2D** **Listening Exercise 1 - Listen to the first line from the 'Other Cultures' text.**
Notice that some syllables are stressed and others are *un*stressed.

The symbol /ə/ is shown above the *un*stressed (*weak*) syllables and words. The *stressed syllables* are underlined.

/ə/   /ə/   /ə/   /ə/   /ə/   /ə//ə//ə/ /ə//ə/   /ə/   /ə/

<u>What</u> is <u>cul</u>ture? <u>Cul</u>ture <u>means</u> the <u>way</u> of <u>liv</u>ing of a par<u>tic</u>ular <u>group</u> of <u>peo</u>ple.

- You can see that English pronunciation consists of stressed and unstressed syllables.
- You can see how often the unstressed sound /ə/ can occur in spoken English.
- Notice the words, '*the*', '*of*', and '*a*' have a weak sound. They contain the sound /ə/.

Read the following information before doing the exercises below:

In spoken English, words with **stressed** syllables tend to occur with *a regular rhythm*, similar to the beat in music.

In music, some sounds are **l o n g** and **loud**;
some sounds are short and soft.

In spoken English, stressed words *(words with stressed syllables)* are spoken more **clearly** and **loudly** than the other words in the sentence. Stressed words convey the main message of the speaker.

Words that do *not* carry the main message of the speaker are unstressed.
The *un*stressed syllables are reduced to fit between the stressed syllables.
This means they are spoken quickly and softly.

The important thing to remember is that in spoken English, only words that give *important information* are *stressed* by the speaker.

👂 **2D** **Listening Exercise 2 - Listen to the first line from the 'Other Cultures' text again.**

Practise the rhythm by *clapping your hands* on the *stressed syllables* marked with an arrow.

(You will notice a short pause at the end of the question.)

↓   ↓   ↓   ↓   ↓   ↓   ↓   ↓   ↓

What is **cul**ture? **Cul**ture **means** the **way** of **liv**ing of a **par**ticular **group** of **peo**ple.

Can you hear that there is about the same length of time between the stressed syllables?

🎧 **2D Listening Exercise 3**

Stressing _every_ word (or syllable) in a sentence can make a person sound _unfriendly or angry_ to listeners. Listen to the speaker stressing _every_ word. This sounds very <u>_unnatural_</u> to English listeners:

↓ ↓ ↓ ↓ ↓ ↓ ↓ ↓ ↓ ↓ ↓ ↓ ↓ ↓ ↓ ↓ ↓ ↓ ↓
Cul/ture/ means /the/ way /of/ liv/ing /of/ /a/ /par/ti/cu/lar/ group /of/ peo/ple.

Incorrect stress patterns can make it difficult for listeners to understand you.
Remember _stressed_ syllables are in the words that _give information_ – the _content words_.

🎧 **2D** Listening Exercise 4 - Listen to the _correctly stressed sentence_ again.

↓ ↓ ↓ ↓ ↓ ↓ ↓
Culture **means** the **way** of **liv**ing of a particular **group** of **peo**ple.

As you can see, the **stressed** syllables are in the words that **give information**.
(_Words with stressed syllable_ are often referred to as _stressed words_.)
Practise saying the sentence with the correct stress pattern.

> When speaking English, you can help your listeners to understand you by stressing only the important words – the words that give the important information.

Look at the illustration on the right.
The woman is having trouble understanding the speaker.
The man's grammar is correct, so what is the problem?

🎧 **2D Listening Exercise 5 - Listen to the speaker.**

What's the problem?

Discuss the following questions:

1) Why is the listener having trouble understanding the speaker?

2) How can the speaker make his message easier for the listener to understand?

Remember!

- In English, speakers help their listeners _hear_ the important information by _stressing only words with important information._

- Words such as _the, of, for, a, from, and, to,_ are generally _reduced_. This means they are spoken quickly and softly – they are _unstressed or weak._

Now read what the speaker said.
Which are the *important words* that the speaker _should_ have *stressed*?

Underline the words in the speaker's message
that you think the speaker should stress to
make his message clear.

> *I'd like you to meet the manager of the department for cultural education.*

2D   Listening Exercise 6

Listen again. This time the speaker *stresses only the important words*.
Did you underline the correct words? Check your answers on page 131.

If necessary, listen again. Notice that the stressed words contain stressed syllables;
the unstressed words have a weak sound and are spoken quickly (reduced).

Part 3 - Extending the topic

3A Listen to the extended text on 'Other Cultures'.

Notice that the speaker stresses some words but not other words.

Other Cultures

What is culture? Culture means the way of living of a particular group of people.
People from different cultures grow up with different customs, beliefs and values.
For example, if you travel from one country to another, you'll probably find the
people do some things very differently to the ways you are familiar with in your
culture. Culture is usually passed from parents to children for many generations
so people sometimes believe that their culture is the only correct way to live.

Do you think everyone in the world should do things as you do them in your culture or
are you open-minded about other customs? Many people believe that learning about
other cultures can be educational and rewarding.

Learning about another culture doesn't have to mean agreeing with the customs, beliefs
and values of that culture. However, by being tolerant of other people's customs,
problems between people of different cultures may be prevented. *Intercultural
problems often occur because people *don't know* about the customs and beliefs
of people from other cultures. People may not be aware that behaviour that
is acceptable in their culture may be offensive in another culture. By *knowing*
about the customs and values of the people we meet, we can avoid intercultural
misunderstandings and problems.

Can you think of a custom of your culture that travellers would need to know about,
if they were going to travel to your native country or meet people from your culture?

*Note: 'Intercultural' means 'between different cultures'.

3B Extending your vocabulary

Find and underline the following words in the last two paragraphs of the text on the 'Other Cultures' text on the previous page.

tolerant	prevented	occur	(be) aware (of)
avoid	acceptable	offensive	behaviour

Match the above words from the text with the correct meaning listed below. The first one has been done as an example.

1) stay away from   _avoid_   5) happen   _____

2) OK, good, appropriate   _____   6) know about/understand   _____

3) bad, insulting   _____   7) stopped before it happens   _____

4) open-minded, willing to
listen to other opinions   _____   8) way of doing, acting   _____

🎧 **3B**   Listen and check your answers to 3B. Repeat the words after the speaker.

Part 4 - Analysing stressed and unstressed syllables

◀◀ **Replay Part 3B and listen to the words again.**

Can you hear that some syllables are *stressed* and other syllables are *unstressed*?

/ə/ eg. a<u>void</u>	acceptable	offensive	tolerant
occur	aware	prevented	behaviour

Underline the syllable which has the **main** stress in each word.
Write /ə/ above the *unstressed* syllables, as in the example.

- Check the words in a dictionary to see if you are correct.
   Note: Some dictionaries use /ɪ/ to indicate some unstressed syllables
      eg. *prevented* may be shown as /prɪventəd/ or /prəventəd/.

- You can also check your answers on page 131.

   (When checking a word in your dictionary, don't be confused by symbols
   used to represent other sounds in the word. Focus on the symbol /ə/ in this unit.
   The other symbols will be explained later in the book).

Part 5 - Understanding the link between spoken and written English

The unstressed (weak) sound /ə/ can be represented <u>in writing</u> by *any vowel letter*.
Look at the following examples:

letter **a** = /ə/	letter **e** = /ə/	letter **i** = /ə/	letter **o** = /ə/	letter **u** = /ə/
↓	↓	↓	↓	↓
umbrella	open	opposite	reason	success

> Remember your dictionary can help you to learn the correct *pronunciation* of new words as well as the meaning.

Part 6 – Spelling Check - Dictation

𝄞 **Listen to the *Other Cultures* text again.**

✎ **Complete the text with the correct words.** (Pause the recording to write the words.)

What is culture? Culture means the way of living of a _____ group of people.

People from _____ cultures grow up with different _____, beliefs and values.

For example, if you _____ from one country to _____, you'll probably find the

people do some things very differently to the ways you are _____ with in your

culture. Culture is usually passed from parents to children for many _____ so

people sometimes believe that their culture is the only _____ way to live.

Check your answers by comparing this page with the *Other Cultures* text in Part 1A.

Part 7 - Listening Practice – Questions

𝄞 **7A Listen and complete the questions.** (Pause the recording after each question.)

✎ **Write the words you hear.**

1) _____ ?

2) _____ ?

3) _____ ?

Check your answers on page 131 and make corrections if necessary.

7B ◀◀ Replay Part 7A and listen to the questions again.

- Which words does the speaker stress to signal the *important information*?
- Which words are more difficult to hear because they are *un*stressed?

Check your answers on page 131 before continuing.

Part 8 - Review - Understanding English Stress and Rhythm

Word Stress

- Spoken words contain *syllables*. A syllable is formed by the linking of individual sounds within a word to form one unit of unbroken sound. A word can contain one or more syllables.

- In spoken English, some syllables in words are spoken more clearly or strongly than others. Strong or prominent sounds are called *stressed* syllables.
  The weaker or reduced sounds are called *unstressed* syllables and are usually represented in dictionaries by the symbol /ə/. This sound and its symbol /ə/ is called the *schwa*.

Stress within utterances

- In spoken English, words which give **important information** contain *stressed* syllables. These are generally **content words** ie. nouns (things), verbs (actions) adjectives (describers).

  Words which *don't* carry the main message of the speaker (ie. structure words like *the, of, a*), are generally *unstressed.* These unstressed words are spoken softly and quickly.

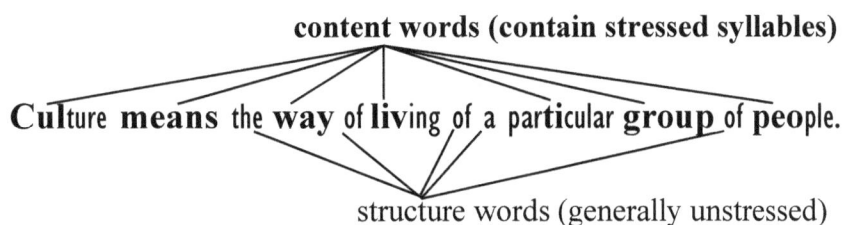

content words (contain stressed syllables)

Culture means the way of living of a particular group of people.

structure words (generally unstressed)

- **In English, not all words are given equal time**.
  The stressed syllables tend to occur with a regular rhythm (like the beat in music).
  The *un*stressed syllables are shortened to fit between the stressed syllables.
  (Note that the regularity of speech rhythm may be affected by the context of the conversation.
  For example, fast informal speech may not have the same regular rhythm of slow careful speech.)

- **Stress in utterances helps the listener** *focus* **on the** *important information.*
  Putting stress on *every* word can make a person sound *unfriendly or angry* to English listeners, as well as making it difficult for listeners to hear the important information.
  English speakers stress 'information words' only.

- In **writing,** the weak or unstressed sound /ə/ can be represented by *any vowel letter*.

A good dictionary can help you to learn the correct *pronunciation* of new words, as well as the meaning.

Part 9 - Pronouncing the letters 'th' correctly

👂 **Listen to the following sentences. Notice how the letters 'th' are pronounced.**

> *They thanked their mothers. Then they thanked both brothers.*

In spoken English, the letters '*th*' can be pronounced in two different ways.

1) 'th' can be pronounced *without using the voice box.* eg. *think, thank, both,*
   Put your tongue between your teeth. Blow air gently between your tongue and teeth.
   Say: 'thank'. This quiet, voiceless sound is represented by the symbol /θ/.

2) 'th' can be pronounced *using the voice box* as in the words *then, they, their.*
   When the voice is used to say 'th', it is represented by the symbol /ð/.

$$ \text{ð/} \quad \text{/θ/} \quad \text{/ð/} \quad \text{/ð/} \quad \text{/ð/} \quad \text{/ð/} \quad \text{/θ/} \quad \text{/θ/} \quad \text{/ð/} $$
They thanked their mothers. Then they thanked both brothers.

'th' may be represented with different symbols in your dictionary, so check the words in *your* dictionary now.

9A

/θ/ **Put your hand on your voice box (as in the picture) and pronounce the following words slowly:**

think, thank, both

You should <u>not</u> be able to feel your voice box vibrating when you say the 'th' part of the word correctly, as /θ/ is a voiceless sound.

/ð/ **Put your hand on your voice box and say the following words slowly:**

then, they, their

If you are pronouncing 'th' correctly, as /ð/, you <u>will</u> feel your voice box vibrating. /ð/ is a voiced sound.

> Some sounds are made in your 'voice box' inside your neck. These sounds are called 'voiced sounds'.
>
> Some sounds are made without using your 'voice box'. They are called 'voiceless' or 'unvoiced' sounds.

👂 **9B Listen to the pronunciation of the letters 'th' in following sentences.**

> Do you <u>th</u>ink everyone in <u>th</u>e world should do <u>th</u>ings as you do <u>th</u>em in your culture or are you open-minded about o<u>th</u>er customs? Most people believe <u>th</u>at learning about o<u>th</u>er cultures can be educational and rewarding.

- Which words contain /θ/ and which contain /ð/?
- Check your answers (p.131) then practise reading the sentences with the correct pronunciation of 'th'.

Distinguishing between sounds /s/, /t/ and /θ/

Some students of English have difficulty distinguishing between the sounds /s/, /t/ and /θ/.

9C   Listen to the underlined consonant sounds. Can you hear the difference?

/θ/ mou<u>th</u>	/θ/ <u>th</u>ing	/θ/ <u>th</u>ought	/θ/ <u>th</u>in
/s/ mou<u>s</u>e	/s/ <u>s</u>ing	/t/ <u>t</u>aught	/t/ <u>t</u>in

Distinguishing between sounds /s/, /t/ and /θ/ in fluent speech

<u>Underline</u> the words which are different in sentences a) and b) below.
The first one has been done as an example.

9D   Listen and tick ☑ the sentence you hear, a) or b).

1) ☐ a) He said <u>something</u> better than them.
    ☐ b) He said <u>some sing</u> better than them

2) ☐ a) Did you see the little boy's mouth?
    ☐ b) Did you see the little boy's mouse?

3) ☐ a) He thought for a long time.
    ☐ b) He taught for a long time.

4) ☐ a) I'd like to order two thin boxes, please.
    ☐ b) I'd like to order two tin boxes, please.

Check your answers on page 131 before continuing.

Now practise pronouncing the sentences correctly. Work with a partner.

- One person should say sentence a) or b).

- The other person should decide which sentence he/she hears.

Pronouncing names correctly

It is important to know the correct pronunciation of the names of people you meet regularly and the correct pronunciation of the towns and cities in your area.

As you have learnt, it is necessary to know how many syllables a word contains in order to be able to pronounce it correctly. It is also important to know which syllable is stressed.

PEOPLE

Write the names of people in your class (or people you work with) in the space on the right.

Ask them to pronounce their name slowly.
Mark the syllables and the stress.
Check with them that you are pronouncing their names correctly.

PLACES

Write the names of places in your area in the space on the left.

Ask a person who lives locally to pronounce the name slowly.

Mark the syllables and stress.
Check with them that you are pronouncing the place names correctly.

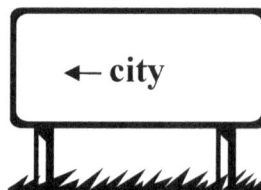

← city

Unit 4
City Living

In this unit you will: In this unit you will:

- Discuss the topic of City Living.

- Practise distinguishing between the sounds /ɪ/ as in 'ship' and /iː/ as in 'sheep'.

- Practise pronouncing the sounds /ɪ/ and /iː/ in fluent speech.

- Analyse the link between spoken and written English ie. ways of spelling the sounds /ɪ/ and /iː/.

- Learn how speakers make their meaning clear in spoken communication.

Preliminary Listening

🕮 **Listen to the vowel sounds in the following words. Can you hear the difference?**

/ɪ/ ship	/ɪ/ bins	/ɪ/ fit	/ɪ/ hit
/iː/ sheep	/iː/ beans	/iː/ feet	/iː/ heat

Note: The sound /ɪ/ as in the word 'ship', and /iː/ as in 'sheep', may be represented with different symbols in your dictionary, so check the words in <u>your</u> dictionary now. What symbols does your dictionary use?

Part 1 - Introduction to the topic

Think about the topic before turning the page to read and listen to the text.

The speaker will talk about *City Living*. What do you think the speaker will say?

☐ a) Many country people think city living is <u>artificial</u>.

or

☐ b) Many country people think city living is <u>expensive</u>.

Check your answer by listening to Part 1A.

Unit 4 – City Living

In Part 1, focus on *what* the speaker says about the topic.
You will focus on *how* words are pronounced in Part 2.

👂 **1A   Listen as you read the text about *City Living*.**

City Living

Today most people in the world live in or near a city. This is possibly because big cities provide <u>opportunities</u> for business and study which aren't always available in the country. For example, when country children reach their <u>teens</u>, parents begin to see that their small country town may not fill the educational and employment needs of their children as easily as the city. So they begin to think about the things that need to be done to prepare for the future. This may involve the whole family leaving the country to live nearer the city, or the children leaving their family to study at university or find a job in the city. But many country people feel <u>ill at ease</u> about leaving their small country town for a new life in the big city. This feeling may be because they have <u>preconceived</u> beliefs about city living.

A recent study <u>revealed</u> the beliefs that some country people had about city living. For instance, some country people said they believed that city living would be <u>artificial</u> compared to country living - 'too much concrete and not enough green', 'too many street signs and not enough trees'. They also believed that, even if city people <u>frequently</u> visit the <u>gym</u>, they're still not as <u>fit</u> as country people. In general, country people think the city is a <u>risky</u> place to live.

Well - what do you think of these beliefs about city living? Do you agree or disagree?

🖊 **1B   Write the underlined words in the text next to the correct meaning below.**
The first one has been done as an example.

1) nervous/uneasy   *ill at ease*   6) often   _____

2) good chances   _____   7) not natural   _____

3) age between 13 to 19 years   _____   8) dangerous   _____

4) showed   _____   9) healthy/strong   _____

5) judged before knowing facts   _____   10) building for indoor
                                                                  sport and exercise   _____

👂   **1B   Listen and check your answers to 1B. Repeat the words after the speaker.**

👥   **1C   Now discuss the following questions:**

1) Why do many people live near the city?

2) What beliefs do some country people have about city living?

Part 2 – Focus on Pronunciation

2A Listen to the following words from the text.

Which words contain the sound /ɪ/ as in *ship*? Which contain the sound /iː/ as in *sheep*?

th<u>i</u>s	b<u>u</u>siness	t<u>ee</u>ns	l<u>i</u>ving	l<u>ea</u>ving	f<u>i</u>ll	f<u>ee</u>l
rev<u>ea</u>led	bel<u>ie</u>ve	<u>i</u>s	<u>ea</u>se	pr<u>e</u>conc<u>ei</u>ved	artif<u>i</u>cial	
g<u>y</u>m	f<u>i</u>t	th<u>e</u>se	fr<u>e</u>quently	r<u>i</u>sky		

◀◀ **Replay the recording of 2A. Pause the recording after each word.**
Write the words in the correct lists below, according to the <u>underlined</u> sound.

1) Sound /ɪ/ as in the word ship	2) Sound /iː/ as in the word sheep
th<u>i</u>s	*t<u>ee</u>ns*

Check your answers on page 132 before continuing.

2B - Syllables and Word Stress - Revision

◀◀ **Replay Part 2A and listen to all the words again.**
How many syllables are there in each word? Listen carefully!

Write them in the correct lists below.
<u>Underline</u> the stressed syllables in words with two or more syllables.

words with one syllable	*words with two syllables*	*words with three syllables*	*words with four syllables*

Check your answers on page 132 before continuing.

* For information on the pronunciation of words with 'ed' endings, see Unit 5, Part 2B.

In Part 3, focus on *what* the speaker says about the topic.
Words with the sounds /ɪ/ and /iː/ will be analysed in Part 4.

Part 3 - Extending the topic

🎧 **3A   Listen to the extended text on *'City Living'*.**

City Living

Today most people in the world live in or near a city. This is possibly because big cities provide opportunities for business and study which aren't always available in the country. For example, when country children reach their teens, parents begin to see that their small country town may not fill the educational and employment needs of their children as easily as the city. So they begin to think about the things that need to be done to prepare for the future. This may involve the whole family leaving the country to live nearer the city, or the children leaving their family to study at university or find a job in the city. But many country people feel ill at ease about leaving their small country town for a new life in the big city. This feeling may be because they have preconceived beliefs about city living.

A recent study revealed the beliefs that some country people had about city living. For instance, some country people said they believed that city living would be artificial compared to country living - 'too much concrete and not enough green', 'too many street signs and not enough trees'. They also believed that, even if city people frequently visit the gym, they're still not as fit as country people. In general, country people think the city is a risky place to live.

Well - what do you think of these beliefs about city living?
Do you agree or disagree?

People may get the idea that the city is a risky place to live through images seen in movies in which criminals and thieves are frequently seen on city streets. The media may also depict the city as an unfriendly place, where people are so busy they don't even have time to greet each other. Of course, many city people would completely disagree with these beliefs about city living and suggest that these media images are very deceiving. In fact, millions of people feel completely at ease living in the city and believe it to be much more interesting and convenient than the country. Really, it would be difficult for them to imagine living anywhere else.

3B Extending your vocabulary

✏️   **Find and <u>underline</u> the following words in the <u>last paragraph</u> of text above.**

im<u>a</u>ges	cr<u>i</u>minals	th<u>ie</u>ves	m<u>e</u>dia	dep<u>i</u>ct
gr<u>ee</u>t	dece<u>i</u>ving	complet<u>e</u>ly	at <u>ea</u>se	conv<u>e</u>nient

Match the words you have underlined in the text with the correct meaning listed below.
One has been done as an example.

1) pictures or ideas   *images*   6) feel comfortable   _____

2) people guilty of crime   _____   7) say hello   _____

3) show, describe   _____   8) people who steal   _____

4) television, radio, newspapers _____   9) easy, handy   _____

5) causing false belief   _____   10) totally, 100%   _____

3B   **Listen and check your answers to 3B. Repeat the words after the speaker.**

Part 4 - Analysing the sounds

Replay 3B and listen to the pronunciation of the stressed syllable in each word.
(If necessary, pause the recording after each word).
Write the words in the correct columns below, then check your answers on page 132.

1) Words with the sound /ɪ/ (as in ship)	2) Words with the sound /iː/ (as in sheep)
images	

Part 5 - Understanding the link between spoken and written English

Spelling Lists - Ways of *spelling the sound* /ɪ/ (as in the word sh**i**p)

i	y	u & ui	other
live images city this	gym symbol	busy build	pretty women

Spelling Lists - Ways of *spelling the sound* /iː/ (as in the word sh**ee**p)

         * A general spelling rule is: Put 'i' before 'e', except after 'c'.

ea	ee	e	ie*	ei*	i	'y' as word ending
leave reach reveal	see teens feel	these equal media	believe piece thieves	deceive preconceive receive	police deteriorate experience	city easy quality really Also pronounced as the short sound /ɪ/ in some varieties of English.

Part 6 - Spelling Check – Dictation

🎧 **Listen to the City Living text again**

✏️ **Complete the text with the correct words.** (Pause the recording to write the words.)

> City Living
>
> Today most _____ in the world _____ in or near a city. This is possibly because
> big cities provide opportunities for _____ and study which aren't always available
> in the country. For example, when country children _____ their _____, parents
> begin to _____ that their small country town may not _____ the educational and
> employment _____ of their children as _____ as the city. So they begin to think
> about the things that _____to be done to prepare for the future. This may involve the
> whole family _____ the country to _____ nearer the city, or the children leaving
> their family to study at university or find a job in the city. But many country people feel
> _____ at _____ about leaving their small country town for a new life in the big city.
> This _____ may be because they have preconceived _____ about city living.

Part 7 - Listening Practice – Stress within utterances

🎧 **7A** **Listen to someone asking questions about city living.**

✏️ **Write the words you hear.** (Pause the recording after each question.)

1)_____?

2) _____ *most*_____?

3)_____ *least* _____?

Check your answers on page 132 before continuing.

In Unit 3 you learnt about stress within utterances. Speakers usually stress *content words* (nouns, main verbs and adjectives) because these words signal the important information.

7B ◀◀ **Replay 7A and listen to the questions again.**
Can you *hear* that the content words are stressed?
<u>Underline</u> **the words in each question (above) that are stressed by the speaker.**

Check your answers on page 133 before continuing.

> As well as stressing content words, speakers can choose to highlight a *particular part*
> of a sentence or question more than the rest of the message.
> They can choose to make a particular part of the message *more prominent*.

Making the *most important* information *prominent*

In this section you will learn about ***prominent*** words. These are the words that the speaker wants to make the *most* important or prominent in a message. A prominent word is generally one of the stressed words. (***Prominent*** words are also called *focus* words.)

The prominent word or words signal the ***most important*** piece of information to the listener.

7C ◄◄ Replay 7A and listen to the questions again.
Decide which word (of those you have underlined) is made the <u>most</u> prominent by the speaker in each question.

Draw a box around the most prominent word in each question in 7A.

Check your answers on page 133 before continuing.

Focussing attention on the main point

In *written* messages, writers can <u>underline</u> important words, write them in *italics,* **bold letters** or in CAPITALS to make sure the reader sees the main point.

In *spoken* English, speakers focus the listener's attention on the *most* important part of the message by making some words more noticeable or ***prominent.***

Speakers make words *prominent* by saying them *louder* and *clearer* than the other words, and by having a *pitch movement* in their voice (up or down) when they say the prominent word.

The words a speaker makes prominent will depend on the context of the conversation.

7D Listen to the explanation and examples.

• **New information is generally made prominent. Listen:**

(Words with stressed syllables are <u>underlined</u>. Prominent words are in a box.)

'He's going to Greece.'

• **In following sentences, the focus may be on whichever words the speaker wants to make prominent. Listen:**

'Who else is going?'

• **A speaker can make more than one word in an utterance prominent. Listen:**

'It was my idea not yours.'

Distinguishing between the sounds /ɪ/ and /iː/ in fluent speech

Underline the words which are different in sentences a) and b) below. The first one has been done as an example.

7E **Listen and tick ☑ the sentence, a) or b) that you hear.**

1) ☐ a) Do they sell <u>bins</u>?
   ☐ b) Do they sell <u>beans</u>?

2) ☐ a) They're living on a boat.
   ☐ b) They're leaving on a boat.

3) ☐ a) Can you see the ship near the rocks?
   ☐ b) Can you see the sheep near the rocks?

4) ☐ a) That was a very good pitch.
   ☐ b) That was a very good peach.

5) ☐ a) You must hit the metal to make it bend.
   ☐ b) You must heat the metal to make it bend.

6) ☐ a) I've never seen this before.
   ☐ b) I've never seen these before.

7) ☐ a) It's easy to slip in here.
   ☐ b) It's easy to sleep in here.

8) ☐ a) Did you fill it?
   ☐ b) Did you feel it?

9) ☐ a) How is he?
   ☐ b) How easy?

Check your answers on page 133 before continuing.

7F **Revision exercise – hearing prominent words**

◀◀ **Replay 7E.** Pause the recording after each sentence.

Listen and draw a ▢box around the word or words the speaker makes *most* prominent in each utterance.

Check your answers on page 133 before continuing.

Now practise pronouncing the sentences. Work with a partner.

• One person should say sentence a) or b).

• The other person should decide which sentence he/she hears.

Part 8 - Pronouncing place names

🦻 **8A Listen to the English pronunciation of the following places.**

/ɪ/
eg. Man<u>i</u>lla _city_____ Syr<u>i</u>a_____ Gr<u>ee</u>ce _____ L<u>i</u>ma _____

<u>E</u>ngland _____ Madr<u>i</u>d _____ <u>E</u>gypt _____ Qu<u>i</u>to _____

Sw<u>e</u>den _____ L<u>i</u>sbon _____ S<u>y</u>dney _____

Use an atlas to locate the places then answer the questions below.

Which places are cities? Which places are countries?
Write '*country*' or '*city*' next to each place, as in the example above.

8B ◀◀ **Replay 8A.** Which places contain the sound /ɪ/ and which contain the sound /iː/?
Write the correct symbol above the <u>underlined</u> sound in each place name above.
The first one has been done as an example.

Check your answers on page 133 before continuing.

Discuss: Which of the above places would you like to visit?

Using intonation to communicate meaning

Intonation refers to the way the voice goes up and down in pitch when we are speaking.
In English, speakers use intonation in various ways to convey meaning.

In English, meaning depends on *how* something is said, as well as *what* is said.

Giving feedback through intonation

When in conversation, speakers expect to receive
'feedback' from their listeners. This means they expect
to receive some signal about what the listener is thinking.
In English, intonation can be an important indicator of a
speaker's attitude to what has been said. For example, in
the illustration on the right, the man is using rising intonation
to show interest in what has been said. By using rising
intonation, the man is communicating '*I am interested in this.*'

Really?

If he said the same thing with falling intonation, he may sound *un*interested.
The <u>same words</u> can be said with <u>different intonation</u>, producing a <u>different meaning</u>.

Of course, intonation is not the only indication of a person's attitude. The words we use, our facial expression and gestures also contribute to the 'messages' we convey. However, it is important and useful to be able to hear how intonation can contribute to meaning.

8C Listen to the conversation in which friends are talking about their favourite cities.

Where do the speakers use _rising intonation_ to show _surprise or interest_?

Mark the rising intonation with an arrow.

A: If you could live in any city you wished, which city would you pick?

B: That's easy. Madrid.

A: Madrid?

B: Yes, definitely. I think Madrid's a fascinating place.
And which city would you pick?

A: It'd have to be Sydney.

B: Really?

A: Yes – it's always been my dream to live in Sydney.

Check your answers on page 133 before continuing.

8D ◀◀ **Replay the recording of 8C and listen to the conversation again.**

Draw a box around the words that are made most prominent by the speakers.

Check your answers on page 133 before continuing.

Practise the conversation, changing the city names to suit your opinion.

In English there is an expression:

'It's not <u>what</u> you say, it's <u>the way</u> that you say it.'

This means that making our spoken message clear involves more than the words we say. _How_ we say the words in our message can be as important as _what_ we say.

Making your message clear in English involves:

- understanding that not all words are stressed. Only the information words contain stressed syllables.

- making the _most_ important words in the message _prominent_.

- understanding how intonation contributes to meaning. (You will learn more about this.)

Remember:

In spoken English, words which give information contain *stressed* syllables.
These are generally content words ie. nouns (things), verbs (actions) adjectives (describers).

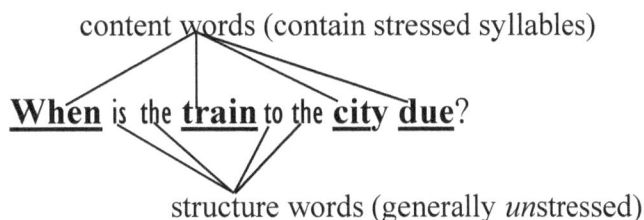

content words (contain stressed syllables)

When is the **train** to the **city** **due**?

structure words (generally *un*stressed)

Words which *don't* carry the main message of the speaker are generally *unstressed*.
Unstressed words are generally spoken softly and quickly.

Part 9 - Making the *most* important part of the message prominent

When saying, '*When is the train to the city due?*', the speaker may make *one* word more *prominent*
than the other words to focus the listener's attention on a particular part of the message.
The speaker will do this to convey a particular meaning.

9A Listen to the following sentences.

Put a box around the word the speaker makes most prominent in each utterance.
Notice how prominence is given to a different word each time.

The first one has been done as an example.

1) When's the train to the city due?
2) When's the train to the city due?
3) When's the train to the city due?
4) When's the train to the city due?

Check your answers on page 133.

By noticing which word is prominent, the listener understands what the speaker is asking about.

9B

Match each sentence above, with the speaker's meaning (below).
One has been done as an example.

a) The speaker wants to know about *when* the train will arrive, not *where* it will arrive. _____
b) The speaker wants to know about trains to the *city*, not trains to the *country*. __1__
c) The speaker wants to know about trains *to* the city, not *from* the city. _____
d) The speaker wants to know about the *train*, not the *bus*. _____

Check your answers on page 133.

Note: In question 4, the word '*to*', generally an unstressed word, is made prominent because it is important to the
message of the speaker, ie. She wants to ask about the train '*to*' the city, not the train '*from*' the city.

Summary – Making the main point prominent

In *written* messages, writers can <u>underline</u> important words, write them *italics* or in CAPITALS to make sure the reader sees the main point.

In *spoken* English, speakers focus the listener's attention on the *most important* part of the message by making some words more noticeable or *prominent*.

The words a speaker makes prominent will depend on the context of the conversation.

New information is generally made prominent.

- **New information is generally made prominent.**

(Words with stressed syllables are <u>underlined</u>.
Prominent words are in a box.)

'He's <u>going</u> to Greece.'

- **In following sentences, the focus (prominence) may be on whichever words the speaker wants to be noticed.**

'Which part of <u>Greece</u>?'

Speakers help their listeners *focus* on the main point by making the *most important words prominent*.

Listeners understand which part of the message contains the most important information by noticing the prominent words.

Unit 5
National Parks

In this unit you will:

- Discuss the topic of 'National Parks'

- Practise identifying the sounds /æ/ (as in p*a*ck) and /ɑ:/ (as in p*a*rk)

- Practise pronouncing the sounds /æ/ and /ɑ:/ in fluent speech

- Analyse the link between spoken and written English
  ie. ways of spelling the sounds /æ/ and /ɑ:/

- Practise identifying and pronouncing the sounds /p/ and /b/

- Learn how intonation is used to communicate meaning

Preliminary Listening

Listen to the vowel sounds in the following words. Can you hear the difference?

/æ/ hat	/æ/ ban	/æ/ pack	/æ/ a lamb
/ɑ:/ heart	/ɑ:/ barn	/ɑ:/ park	/ɑ:/ alarm

Note: The sound /æ/ as in the word 'hat', and /ɑ:/ as in 'heart', may be represented with different symbols in your dictionary, so check the words in your dictionary now. What symbols does your dictionary use?

Part 1 - Introduction to the topic

Think about the topic before turning the page to read and listen to the text.

The speaker will talk about *National Parks*. What do you think the speaker will say?

☐ a) National Parks have been established as tourist attractions.

or

☐ b) National Parks have been established to protect the world's natural marvels.

Check your answer by listening to Part 1A.

In Part 1, focus on *what* the speaker says about the topic.
You will focus on *how* words are pronounced in Part 2.

1A Listen as you read the text about *'National Parks'*.

National Parks

As the world's population has <u>expanded,</u> a lot of land has been cleared for farming, housing and mining. The <u>rapid</u> development of railways, roads and industry into <u>sparsely</u> populated areas, has caused animals and birds to <u>vanish</u> as their natural <u>habitats</u> have been destroyed. Farmers and land developers have often left large areas of land <u>scarred</u> and damaged.

As the <u>mismanagement</u> of large areas of land throughout the world increased, <u>far-sighted</u> people began to see that action was needed to prevent many of the world's animals from vanishing. <u>Campaigns</u> were started to protect the earth's natural environment from further damage. In 1872, Yellowstone National Park, in the United States of America, became the world's first managed National Park. Since that time, National Parks have been established in many other countries to protect the <u>marvels</u> of our natural world.

1B Write the <u>underlined</u> words in the text above next to the correct meaning below.
The first one has been done as an example.

1) having few people   *sparsely*   6) sensible, wise   _____

2) quick   _____   7) homes/places of living   _____

3) badly marked   _____   8) organised action   _____

4) bad management   _____   9) disappear/die   _____

5) increased, become bigger   _____   10) wonderful things   _____

1B Listen and check your answers to 1B. Repeat the words after the speaker.

1C Discuss the following questions.

1) What has happened to the land in some areas as the world's population has expanded?

2) Where was the world's first National Park established?

Part 2 – Focus on Pronunciation

👂 **2A** **Listen to the underlined vowel sound in the following words.** Is it /æ/ or /ɑː/?

exp<u>a</u>nded	r<u>a</u>pid	sp<u>a</u>rsely	v<u>a</u>nish	h<u>a</u>bitats	sc<u>a</u>rred
n<u>a</u>tural	st<u>a</u>rted	beg<u>a</u>n	f<u>a</u>r-sighted	m<u>a</u>rvels	

⏪ **Replay the recording of 2A. Pause the recording after each word.**
✏️ **Write the words in the correct columns below, according to the underlined sound.**

1) Sound /æ/ as in the word *pack*	2) Sound /ɑː/ as in the word *park*
eg. *exp<u>a</u>nded*	

Check your answers on page 134 before continuing.

Pronunciation of words ending with 'ed'

The '*ed*' endings on words (eg. *expand<u>ed</u>*) are sometimes pronounced as an extra syllable.
For example, '*expanded*' has three syllables, /ex pænd əd/.

In some words, the '*ed*' ending becomes part of the preceding syllable. eg. *scarred* = one syllable.

Read the following general rules about 'ed' endings:

1) '**ed**' is pronounced as an extra syllable /əd/ only when added to words which end in /d/ or /t/.
   For example, when '**ed**' is added to the word **ren<u>t</u>**, it is pronounced as /rent̬əd/ (two syllables).
   When '**ed**' is added to the word **men<u>d</u>**, the word men<u>d</u>ed is pronounced as /mend̬əd/.

2) '**ed**' is pronounced as /t/ after the sounds /s / /p/ /f/ /k/ /θ/ /ʃ/ /tʃ/ eg. wi**shed** /wɪʃt/; par**ched** /pɑːtʃt/

3) '**ed**' is pronounced as /d/ after **vowel sounds**, after sounds /m/ /n/ /b/ /z/ /v/ /l/ and the sound /dʒ/,
   as in the word 'damaged', /dæmɪdʒd/

👂 **2B** **Listen to the following words ending with 'ed'.**

✏️ **Write the words in the correct column, then check your answers on page 134.**

~~expanded~~	~~caused~~	~~damaged~~	*populated*	*scarred*	*happened*
far-sighted	*needed*		*established*	*started*	*walked*	*packed*

1) *ed* pronounced as /əd/	2) *ed* pronounced as /t/	3) *ed* pronounced as /d/
expanded		*cau<u>s</u>ed* /kɔːzd/ 's' pronounced /z/ *damaged*

Part 3 - Extending the topic

𝔇 3A **Listen to the extended text on *National Parks*.**

In this section, focus on *what* the speaker says about the topic.
Words with the sounds /æ/ and /ɑ:/ will be analysed in Part 4.

National Parks

As the world's population has expanded, a lot of land has been cleared for farming, housing and mining. The rapid development of railways, roads and industry into sparsely populated areas, has caused animals and birds to vanish as their natural habitats have been destroyed. Farmers and land developers have often left large areas of land scarred and damaged.

As the mismanagement of large areas of land throughout the world increased, far-sighted people began to see that action was needed to prevent many of the world's animals from vanishing. Campaigns were started to protect the earth's natural environment from further damage. In 1872, Yellowstone National Park, in the United States of America, became the world's first managed National Park. Since that time, National Parks have been established in many other countries to protect the marvels of our natural world.

National Parks have now been established all over the world as a strategy to protect our fragile planet. Antarctica, for example, is one of the few places on earth which has not been extensively damaged by man. No-one actually owns Antarctica, although several nations claim parts of it. Today, an Antarctic Treaty aims to protect Antarctica from damage to its fragile land and sea animals.

National Parks provide sanctuaries for animals by banning (or regulating) the fishing and hunting of animals within the parks and by guarding the natural beauty of the area. Sadly, the importance of keeping a balance in the natural world has been shown by the damage done to large areas of natural forest through clearing. As a result of clearing, the land has become parched and barren, causing many native animals to starve; even making the land unsuitable for farming. Man is now beginning to understand the value of caring for the land and the importance of acting in harmony with the natural world. National Parks play an important part in protecting the natural assets of our beautiful planet.

3B Extending your vocabulary

Find and <u>underline</u> the following words in the last two paragraphs of the text above.

---

str<u>a</u>tegy	fr<u>a</u>gile	s<u>a</u>nctuaries	b<u>a</u>nning	gu<u>ar</u>ding
p<u>ar</u>ched	b<u>a</u>rren	st<u>ar</u>ve	h<u>ar</u>mony	<u>a</u>ssets

---

Match the words you have underlined in the text with the correct meaning listed below. One has been done as an example.

1) plan of management   *strategy*   6) die of hunger   _____

2) dried/burnt   _____   7) easily damaged   _____

3) balance, agreement   _____   8) not producing   _____

4) useful, valuable things   _____   9) not allowing   _____

5) places of protection   _____   10) protecting   _____

3B   Listen and check your answers to 3B. Repeat the words after the speaker.

Part 4 - Analysing the sounds

◀◀   Replay 3B and listen to the pronunciation of the stressed syllable in each word. (If necessary, pause the recording after each word).
Write the words in the correct columns below, then check your answers on page 134.

1) Words with the sound /æ/ (as in pack)	2) Words with the sound /ɑ:/ (as in park)
*str**a**tegy*	

Part 5 - Understanding the link between spoken and written English

The *sound* /æ/ is almost always represented in writing by the *letter* 'a'.

l**a**nd   **a**nimals   **a**ction   m**a**n

However, some English words containing the letter 'a' may be pronounced differently in different varieties of English. Some examples are:

Word - Spelling	pronounced with /æ/ (as in *pack*)	pronounced with /ɑ:/ (as in *park*)
last	/læst/	/lɑ:st/
ask	/æsk/	/ɑ:sk/
banana	/bənænə/	/bənɑ:nə/
answer	/ænsə/	/ɑ:nsə/
example	/eksæmpl/	/eksɑ:mpl/

The variation in pronunciation of words with /æ/ or /ɑ:/ (shown above) is generally well known. Therefore, this kind of variation in pronunciation doesn't usually cause communication problems.

Note: The speakers on the audio recording pronounce the words '*example*' and '*answer*' differently.

Part 5 - continued

Spelling Lists - Ways of *spelling the sound* /ɑː/ (as in the word *park*)

ar	a	al	ear
la<u>r</u>ge f<u>ar</u>ming	sp<u>a</u> J<u>a</u>va	c<u>al</u>m p<u>al</u>m	h<u>ear</u>t

Note: In some English accents, notably North American and Scottish, the 'r' in words such as *'ha<u>rd</u>'* and *'sca<u>rr</u>ed'* is clearly pronounced. In other English accents the 'r' is not usually pronounced after the sound /ɑː/.

Part 6 - Spelling Check – Dictation

Listen to the text about National Parks again.

Complete the text with the correct words. (Pause the recording to write the word.)

As the world's population has _____ a lot of _____ has been cleared for farming, housing and mining. The _____ development of railways, roads and industry into sparsely populated areas, has caused animals and birds to _____ as their natural _____ have been destroyed. Farmers and land developers have often left large areas of land _____ and damaged.

As the mismanagement of _____ areas of land throughout the world increased, far-sighted people _____ to see that _____ was needed to prevent many of the world's animals from vanishing. Campaigns were started to protect the earth's _____ environment from further _____. In 1872, Yellowstone National Park, in the United States of America, became the world's first _____ National Park. Since that time, National Parks have been established in many other countries to protect the _____ of our natural world.

Part 7 – Listening Practice - Using intonation in English

Intonation refers to the way the voice goes up and down in pitch when we are speaking.
In English, speakers use intonation in various ways to convey meaning. As intonation is always related to the context in which it is used, it is *not* possible to give a 'rule' which will apply in every situation.

The purpose of this course is to provide some *general* guidelines so that you can become more aware of the general ways in which intonation is used.

In the following sections you will examine how the speakers:

◆ use *rising intonation* to *check information* and show *uncertainty*

◆ use *falling intonation* to *tell facts* or *give information* which they believe is *new to the listener.*

The first time you listen to the conversation in 7A, write in the missing words.
In the following exercise you will examine ways in which *intonation* is used by the speakers.

7A Listen to the conversation between friends about national parks.

Pause the recording to write the words.

Q1) What do you think about National Parks?_____ necessary?

A1) Absolutely - without them many animals'd vanish.

Q2) _____one?

A2) Yes, I've been to Galapagos and that was spectacular.

Q3) Galapagos? _____South America?

A3) No, it's a group of islands off the west coast. It's part of Ecuador.

Q4) Oh I see. _____?

A4) Well, there're no large land animals on Galapagos - but we did get to see
an albatross and that was fantastic.

Q5) Yes, I can imagine….What other places _____?

A5) I'd love to travel to Africa and go on safari and see antelope and black rhino.
That'd be fantastic! - and Antarctica - I think Antarctica'd be spectacular.

Check your answers on page 134 and make corrections if necessary before continuing.

(When you check the answers on the answer page, you will see which words the speakers
make most **prominent** in the conversation. The prominent words are shown within a box.)

Using intonation to indicate 'checking' and 'telling'

◄◄ Replay 7A and listen to the conversation again.

Notice the speakers' intonation in lines Q3, A3 (also shown in the illustration below).

Notice how the speaker uses rising intonation to '*check*' information.

Notice how the speaker uses falling intonation to '*tell*' information.

*Galapagos? Is that
in South America?*

*No, it's a group of islands
off the west coast.
It's part of Ecuador.*

7B - Extension activity – practising intonation

✎ **Using the information on the map below, complete the following information.**

    'Checking'   *'Telling'*

Q) Is Bamff National Park in Africa?   A) No, it's in _____.

Q) Is Akan National Park in Canada?   A) No, it's in _____.

Q) Is Mana Pools National Park in Japan?   A) No, it's in _____.

👥 Check your answers on page 135 then practise the conversation with a partner, using rising intonation in the question (checking) and falling intonation in the reply (telling).

Bamff National Park, Canada

Galapagos National Park, Ecuador

Sarek National Park, Sweden

Akan National Park, Japan

Mana Pool National Park, Africa

Kaziranga National Park, India

Kakadu National Park, Australia

Remember: Intonation patterns are related to the context in which they are used and individual speakers vary in their use of intonation. It is therefore *not* possible to give a 'rule' which will apply in every situation. However, some general guidelines are given below with examples.

Falling intonation is mainly associated with:

- Introducing a topic with questions which begin with, *Who, When, Where, Why, What, How.*

                                  eg. *What do you think about National Parks?*

- 'Telling' new information or facts, making statements   eg. *Without national parks many animals'd vanish.*

Rising intonation is mainly associated with:

- Checking or enquiring further about information already mentioned. This can be done by repeating information with rising intonation   eg. *Galapagos?*
                                  or
by asking a further question with rising intonation   eg. *Is that in South America?*

- Showing interest or surprise   eg. *Really?*

- Offering assistance   eg. *Do you need help?*

While these patterns apply in most cases, there can be variation depending on the speaker and the situation.

Distinguishing between the sounds /æ/ and /ɑ:/ in fluent speech

Underline the words which are different in sentences a) and b) below.
The first one has been done as an example.

7C **Listen and tick** ☑ **the sentence, a) or b), that you hear.**

1) ☐ a) There was a <u>lamb</u> on the road.
   ☐ b) There was <u>alarm</u> on the road.

2) ☐ a) Have they packed the car yet?
   ☐ b) Have they parked the car yet?

3) ☐ a) She wore a white dress with a blue hat.
   ☐ b) She wore a white dress with a blue heart.

4) ☐ a) The dog needs its back checked.
   ☐ b) The dog needs its bark checked.

5) ☐ a) Did you see the cat on the road?
   ☐ b) Did you see the cart on the road?

6) ☐ a) The children watched the match.
   ☐ b) The children watched the march.

Check your answers on page 135 before continuing.

7D Revision Exercises – prominent words

◄◄ Replay 7C and listen to the sentences again.
1) Draw a box around the words the speakers make *most* prominent in each utterance.
2) Listen to the pronunciation of words ending in 'ed' (in sentences 2, 4, 6).
   How many syllables do these words contain?

Check your answers on page 135 before continuing.

Practise pronouncing the sentences. Work with a partner.

- One person should say sentence a) or b).

- The other person should decide which sentence he/she hears.

Part 8 – Intonation – review and practice

As you have learnt, intonation patterns are always related to the context in which they are used. However, there are general patterns of use.

Falling tone is generally associated with:

- *'telling'* something that is news to the hearer
- *introducing a topic* with a question beginning, *Who, When, Where, Why, What, How.*

Rising tone is generally associated with *'referring back'* to something that has already been spoken about. For example by:

- *checking* something that has been said
- *showing interest or surprise* in what has been said
- *offering help* in relation to what has been said (or observed)

8A Read the following conversations. Using the general intonation patterns explained above, mark where the speakers' intonation would rise and fall at the end of each utterance.

Conversation 1 - Frank is telling Jack about his trip.
Jack is uncertain about the location of Kakadu.

I've just come back from a trip to Kakadu. It was spectacular.

Kakadu? Is that in Africa?

Conversation 2 - Jan introduces the topic of Mark's exam.
After Mark tells them his situation, his friend offers help.

How was your exam, Mark?

It was difficult. I need to practise more before the next exam. It starts this afternoon.

This afternoon? Do you need some help to study?

Check your answers on page 135, then practise the conversations.
Ask your teacher or another speaker of English to check your intonation.

Part 9 - Distinguishing between the sounds /p/ and /b/

9A Listen to the consonant sounds in contrast. Can you hear the difference?

/p/ palm	/p/ pair	/p/ pack	/p/ cap
/b/ balm	/b/ bear	/b/ back	b/ cab

- /p/ is made by pressing the lips together, then pushing air quickly forward as you open your lips. <u>Don't</u> use your voice, as /p/ is a voiceless consonant.
  (See Unit 3, 9A for information about voiced and voiceless consonant sounds).

- /b/ is made with same lip movements but also by using your voice. /b/ is a voiced consonant.

Important Pronunciation Notes:

The sound /p/ is produced with a stronger puff of air from between the lips than sound /b/.
Hold some thin tissue paper in front of your face as you say the words in 9A.
If you're pronouncing the sounds correctly, you'll see the paper move more as you pronounce /p/.

When a vowel sound comes before /p/ (a voiceless consonant) it is shorter than when it comes before a voiced consonant such as /b/. For example, c<u>a</u>p has a slightly shorter vowel sound than c<u>a</u>b.

9B <u>Underline</u> the words that are different in sentences a) and b).

1) a) How many pairs did you see?
   b) How many bears did you see?

2) a) Have you packed the car yet?
   b) Have you backed the car yet?

9C Listen and tick ☑ the sentence you hear, a) or b).

Check your answers on page 135 before continuing.

Practise saying the sentences. Work with a partner.

- One person should say sentence a) or b).

- The other person should decide which sentence he/she hears.

Progress Check - One

Exercise 1

🔊 **Listen and tick ☑ the sentence (a) or (b), that you hear.**

The different words in a) and b) have been underlined.

1)
- ☐ a) They <u>matter</u> too much.
- ☐ b) They <u>mutter</u> too much.

2)
- ☐ a) I'll need a <u>cap</u> today.
- ☐ b) I'll need a <u>cab</u> today.

3)
- ☐ a) Did you <u>fill</u> it?
- ☐ b) Did you <u>feel</u> it?

4)
- ☐ a) How many <u>pairs</u> did you see?
- ☐ b) How many <u>bears</u> did you see?

5)
- ☐ a) The children watched the <u>match</u>.
- ☐ b) The children watched the <u>march</u>.

6)
- ☐ a) It's easy to <u>slip</u> in here.
- ☐ b) It's easy to <u>sleep</u> in here.

7)
- ☐ a) He <u>taught</u> for a long time.
- b) He <u>thought</u> for a long time.

Exercise 2

In English, word stress helps the listener to recognise words correctly.

🔊 **Listen and tick ☑ the word (a) or (b) that you hear. The stressed part is <u>underlined</u>.**

1)
- ☐ a) <u>con</u>duct
- ☐ b) con<u>duct</u>

2)
- ☐ a) <u>a</u>vid
- ☐ b) a<u>void</u>

3)
- ☐ a) <u>a</u>sset
- ☐ b) a<u>ssert</u>

4)
- ☐ a) <u>deaf</u>er
- ☐ b) de<u>fer</u>

Exercise 3

🔊 **Listen to the following utterances and write what the speaker says.**

Pause the recording after each line while you write your answer.

1) _____

2) _____

3) _____

4) _____

Exercise 4A

◄◄ **Replay Exercise 3 and listen to the utterances again.**
Mark the rising or falling intonation at the end of each utterance.

Exercise 4B

◄◄ **Replay Exercise 3 and listen to the utterances again.**

What does the intonation tell you about the speaker's meaning?
Write the number of the utterance next to the most suitable meaning below.

- ☐ The speaker is giving new information.
- ☐ The speaker is asking for new information.
- ☐ The speaker is checking information already discussed.
- ☐ The speaker is making an offer of help.

Unit 6
Books and Computers

In this unit you will:

- Discuss the topic of books and computers

- Practise identifying the sounds /ʊ/ (pull) and /u:/ (pool)

- Practise pronouncing the sounds /ʊ/ and /u:/ in fluent speech

- Analyse the link between spoken and written English
  ie. ways of spelling the sounds /ʊ/ and /u:/

- Examine the way words are linked together in fluent, connected speech

Preliminary Listening

Listen to the vowel sounds in the following words. Can you hear the difference?

/ʊ/ pull	/ʊ/ full	/ʊ/ could	/ʊ/ wood
		You could read this.	
/u:/ pool	/u:/ fool	/u:/ cooed	/u:/ wooed

Note: The sound /ʊ/ as in *pull* and /u:/ as in *pool*, may be represented with different symbols in your dictionary, so check the words in your dictionary now. What symbols does your dictionary use?

Part 1 - Introduction to the topic

Think about the topic before turning the page to read and listen to the text.

The speaker will talk about *Books and Computers*. What do you think the speaker will say?

☐ a) Computers are now used by students in most schools and universities.

or

☐ b) Computers are too confusing to be used by young students.

Check your answer by listening to Part 1A.

Unit 6 – Books and Computers

In Part 1, focus on *what* the speaker says about the topic.
You will focus on *how* words are pronounced in Part 2.

1A Listen as you read the text about *Books and Computers*.

Books and Computers

Do you have <u>childhood</u> memories of school rooms full of books or
rooms full of computers? In the past students would look in books for <u>solutions</u>
to their questions, but in schools today, students often look to computers for information.
Computer technology has opened up a whole new world of communication and
educational <u>opportunities</u>. In fact, computers are now used so much it's difficult to
imagine a world without them.

When the first automatic electronic computers were <u>introduced</u> during the 1940's, one
computer <u>took up</u> a whole room and could be used by only a few skilled technicians. Now
computers are so <u>user-friendly</u>, they are <u>routinely</u> used in offices and homes, as well
as schools and universities. In fact, computers have become so <u>crucial</u> to business and
education that some people have the <u>view</u> that modern society is becoming *too* dependent
on computer technology for its own <u>good</u>.

1B Write the underlined words in the text next to the correct meaning below.
The first one has been done as an example.

1) opinion   *view*   6) simple/easy to use   _____

2) period of time as a child   _____   7) good chances   _____

3) answers   _____   8) regularly   _____

4) filled/occupied space   _____   9) very important   _____

5) brought into use for   10) (for its own) benefit   _____
   the first time   _____

1B   Listen and check your answers to 1B. Repeat the words after the speaker.

1C   Now discuss the following questions:

1) When were the first automatic electronic computers first introduced?

2) How have computers changed since they were introduced?

3) What view do some people have about computers?

Part 2 - Focus on Pronunciation

👂 **2A   Listen to the underlined vowel sound in the following words.** (Is it /ʊ/ or /uː/?)

sch<u>oo</u>l	r<u>oo</u>ms	f<u>u</u>ll	comp<u>u</u>ters	b<u>oo</u>ks	st<u>u</u>dents	w<u>ou</u>ld
l<u>oo</u>k	t<u>oo</u>k	c<u>ou</u>ld	f<u>ew</u>	cr<u>u</u>cial	v<u>iew</u>	g<u>oo</u>d

◀◀ **Replay the recording of 2A. Pause the recording after each word.**
Write the words in the correct lists below, according to the underlined sound.
Don't be confused by the spelling. You need to listen to the *pronunciation* of the words!

1) /ʊ/ as in the word *pull*	2) /uː/ as in the word *pool*

Check your answers on page 136 before continuing.

Word Linking in spoken English

When you see English written in a book, the words appear separately, with spaces between them. However, when spoken at natural speed, the words in English sentences are not always heard as separate words, but are linked together. This is called *'connected speech'*.

For example, in spoken English, speakers usually link words that <u>end in a consonant sound</u> with a <u>following word that begins with a vowel sound</u>.

For example: *ope<u>n</u> <u>up</u>'* becomes *open‿up*

👂 **2B   Listen to the *linking of words* in the first sentence from the *Books and Computers* text.**
The linked sounds are shown with the symbol ‿ in between the linked words.

Do you have childhood memories‿of school rooms full‿of books‿or rooms full‿of computers?

Can you hear the way the words are linked?

memories of	becomes	*memories‿of*
books or	becomes	*books‿or*
full of	becomes	*full‿of*

2C   Look at first the paragraph of the text in Part 3A (next page).
Where do you think the words will be linked?

2C Write ⌣ between the words you think may be linked in the <u>first paragraph</u> below.
The first sentence has been done. <u>Check your answers before you listen to Part 3A.</u>

Remember: Words that *end in a consonant sound* are linked to words that *begin with a vowel sound*.

Note: Linking doesn't occur where the speaker pauses between words

Part 3 - Extending the topic

3A Listen to the extended text on *Books and Computers.*

Books and Computers

Do you have childhood memories ⌣ of school rooms full ⌣ of books ⌣ or rooms full ⌣ of computers? In the past students would look in books for solutions to their questions, but in schools today, students often look to computers for information. Computer technology has opened up a whole new world of communication and educational opportunities. In fact, computers are now used so much it's difficult to imagine a world without them.

When the first automatic electronic computers were introduced during the 1940's, one computer took up a whole room and could be used by only a few skilled technicians. Now computers are so user-friendly they are routinely used in offices and homes, as well as schools and universities. In fact, computers have become so crucial to business and education that some people have the view that modern society is becoming *too* dependent on computer technology for its own good.

Some people view computers as very useful tools for communication and research as there's a huge amount of information available through the internet. These people believe computers will improve opportunities for the future. Others, however, say they'd still prefer to look in books for information as the internet is much too time – consuming and very confusing. They believe people should consider the following issues about the use of computers.

Are children reading fewer books due to computers?
Are computers too time-consuming for children, as well as adults?
Will computers completely replace books in schools and universities of the future?
Will computers reduce or improve employment opportunities for future youth?

3B Extending your vocabulary

Find and <u>underline</u> the following words in the <u>last two paragraphs</u> of the text above.

tools	huge	time-consuming	confusing	issues
	due (to)	reduce	improve	youth

Unit 6 – Books and Computers

✎ **Match the words you have underlined in the text with the correct meaning listed below.** One has been done as an example.

1) helpful instruments *tools*

2) very big, great _____

3) decrease, make less _____

4) using a lot of time _____

5) questions, problems _____

6) difficult to understand _____

7) make better _____

8) because of (something) _____

9) young people _____

👂 **3B Listen and check your answers to 3B. Repeat the words after the speaker.**

Part 4 - Analysing the sounds /uː/ and /juː/

In many words containing the sound /uː/, the sound /j/ precedes /uː/.
This is shown in many dictionaries as /juː/ (pronounced like the word *'you'*).

👂 **4A Listen and compare the pronunciation of /uː/ and /juː/ in the following words:**

do /duː/ - *due* /djuː/
fool /fuːl/ - *fuel* /fjuːl/

👂 **4B Listen to the following words.**

✎ Write the symbol /uː/ or /juː/ above the underlined sound in the words.

/uː/	/juː/							
tools	huge	reduce	consuming	issues	confusing	improve	due	youth

Check your answer on page 137 before continuing.

Remember: If you are unsure of the pronunciation of a new word, take the time to check your dictionary!

Part 5 - Understanding the link between spoken and written English

Spelling Lists - Ways of *spelling the sound /ʊ/* (as in the word *pull*)

u	oo	ou	other spellings
put	good	could	woman
full	book	should	

Spelling Lists - Ways of *spelling the sound /uː/* (as in the word *pool*)

u & ui	oo	o	other spellings
rule fruit	tool	do	grew
solution juice	school	move	issue

Part 6 - Spelling Check – Dictionary

🔊 **Listen to the *Books and Computers* text again.**

✎ **Complete the text with the correct words.** (Pause the recording to write the words.)

Books and Computers

Do you have _____ memories of school rooms full of _____ or rooms _____ of computers? In the past students _____ look in books for solutions to their questions, but in schools today, _____ often look to computers for information. Computer technology has opened up a whole _____ world or communication and educational opportunities. In fact, computers are now _____ so much it's difficult to imagine a world without them.

When the first automatic electronic computers were introduced during the 1940's, one computer _____ up a whole room and could be used by only a few skilled technicians. Now computers are so user-friendly, they are _____ used in offices and homes, as well as schools and universities. In fact, computers have become so _____ to business and education that some people have the _____ that modern society is becoming *too* dependent on computer technology for its own _____.

Check your answers by comparing this page with the *Books and Computers* text, Part 1A.

Part 7 - Listening Practice

🔊 **7A Listen to someone asking questions relating to *Books and Computers*.**

✎ **Complete the questions. Write contractions where you hear them.**

Q 1) _____too time-consuming?

Q 2) _____reduce or increase employment in the future?

Q 3) _____completely replace books in the future?

Check your answers on page 137 before continuing.

7B More about connected speech

◄◄ **Replay 7A and listen to the questions again.**
   As you listen, notice the way words are linked.   **(Answers, page 137)**

Notice where words <u>ending with a consonant sound</u> are linked to words <u>beginning with a vowel</u>.

Notice that *'computers will'* becomes contracted to *computers'll*.

Notice that words such as *'are'*, *'the'*, *'or'* are *unstressed*. They contain the sound /ə/.

If necessary, revise contractions in Unit 2, Part 8A.
If necessary, revise unstressed syllables in Unit 3, Part 2D & Unit 3, Part 8.

More about word linking - consonant sound with consonant sound

Linking also occurs between words when *the final consonant sound of a word is the same as the first sound of the following word.* For example, the *'s'* sound in bus⌣stop is linked.

7C Exercise 1 - Listen to the linking in the following question.

'Do you think⌣computers are too time-consuming?'

Can you hear that the sound /k/ in 'thin<u>k</u>' and the /k/ sound in '<u>c</u>omputers' are linked?

7C Exercise 2 - Listen to the following examples.

1) You loo<u>k</u>⌣<u>c</u>ool.

2) I like thi<u>s</u>⌣<u>s</u>ong!

3) Is it the righ<u>t</u>⌣<u>t</u>une?

In the examples above, the *same* consonant *sound* ends one word and begins the next word. The <u>linking sound</u> is usually pronounced only *once*, but a little longer than usual.

Practise saying the sentences in 7C, using the same linking between the consonant sounds as the speaker.

Distinguishing between /ʊ/, /u:/ and /ju:/ in fluent speech

7D Listen to the following sentences and number the sentences as you hear them.

The first sentence you hear has been numbered as an example. 1

☐ a) How do you spell '<u>full</u>'?

☐ b) How do you spell '<u>fool</u>'?

1 c) How do you spell '<u>fuel</u>'?

☐ d) They <u>could</u> .

☐ e) They <u>cooed</u>.

☐ f) They <u>queued</u>.

Check your answers on page 137.

Practise pronouncing the sentences correctly. Work with a partner.

- One person should say sentence a), b), c), d), e) or f).

- The other person should decide which sentence he/she hears.

Part 8 - Connected Speech - Review

In written English, words can be seen separately, with spaces between them on a page. However, in spoken language, the words of a fluent speaker are not always heard as separate, distinct words but are often linked together into groups of words.

When speaking in a natural, fluent, conversational way, English speakers (including educated speakers) contract and link words to help the smooth flow of speech.

Groups of words, which express a particular thought or idea are usually spoken as one piece of information, without long pauses between the individual words. This is called **connected speech**.

In Unit 6 you have learnt some features of connected speech in English. For example:

- Words ending with a <u>consonant</u> sound and followed by words starting with a <u>vowel</u> sound are usually linked.

  eg. loo**k** <u>o</u>ut   look̑out.

- Words ending with a <u>consonant</u> sound are usually linked to words starting with the <u>same consonant sound</u>. The sound is pronounced only once, but a little longer.

  eg. bu<u>s</u> <u>s</u>top   bus̑stop

8A   **Look at the conversation below.**
    Mark where the speakers would link words in fluent speech. .

What time is Susan arriving?

At ten o'clock in the morning.

Check your answers on page 137.

Practise saying the sentences fluently by linking the words.

In Unit 7, you will learn more about connected speech.
There is a complete summary on connected speech at the end of Unit 7.

Unit 7
Health and Happiness

In this unit you will:

- Discuss the topic of Health and Happiness

- Practise distinguishing between the sounds /e/ (in m*e*n) and /æ/ (in m*a*n)

- Practise pronouncing the sounds in fluent speech

- Analyse the link between spoken and written English ie. ways of spelling the sounds /e/ and /æ/

yang

yin

- Examine the linking of words in connected speech

- Examine ways of pronouncing the letter 'c'

Preliminary Listening

👂 **Listen to the vowel sounds in the following words. Can you hear the difference?**

/e/ bet	/e/ said *Did you hear what he said?*	/e/ spend	/e/ ten **10**
/æ/ bat	/æ/ sad	/æ/ spanned 20th century 21st century	/æ/ tan

Note: The sound /e/ as in *bet* and /æ/ as in *bat*, may be represented with different symbols in your dictionary, so check the words in <u>your</u> dictionary now. What symbols does your dictionary use?

Part 1 - Introduction to the topic

Think about the topic before turning the page to read and listen to the text.

The speaker will talk about *Health and Happiness*. What do you think the speaker will say?

☐ a) Balanced living is necessary for health and happiness.

or

☐ b) Wealth and education are necessary for health and happiness.

Check your answer by listening to Part 1A.

In Part 1, focus on *what* the speaker says about the topic.
You will focus on *how* words are pronounced in Part 2.

👂 **1A Listen as you read the text about *Health and Happiness*.**

Health and Happiness

yang ☯ *yin*

Health <u>experts</u> suggest that to stay healthy and happy, it's important to keep our lives in <u>balance</u>. Chinese philosophy, which has <u>spanned</u> thousands of years, uses the principles of *yin* and *yang* to explain the importance of balance in life. Explained simply, *yang* represents the active <u>elements</u> of the universe, whereas the *yin* represents the <u>passive</u> elements. This expresses the importance of balance in all aspects of living. Today health experts agree that it's important to have a balanced life. For example, they've said it's necessary to have a balance between work and rest and to have a balanced exercise program. However, I'm sure you'd agree that in our busy world it's not always easy to get and keep balance in our lives.

Due to business or study <u>deadlines</u>, many people work to <u>excess</u>; leaving little time at the end of their busy day to <u>spend</u> with family and friends. They eat fast-food and don't get enough rest or <u>recreation</u> and then suffer badly from the effects of <u>stress</u>. It's sad that this situation often happens when people believe that <u>access</u> to wealth is the answer to happiness instead of understanding the importance of balanced living.

✏️ **1B Write the underlined words in the text next to the correct meaning below.**
The first one has been done as an example.

1) parts, units   *elements*   7) mental tension   _____

2) people with special knowledge   _____   8) the way into   _____

3) not active   _____   9) time limits   _____

4) use time   _____   10) leisure time   _____

5) extended over time   _____   11) too much, more
                                                           than necessary   _____

6) harmony, having equal amounts   _____

👂 **1B Listen and check your answers to 1B. Repeat the words after the speaker.**

👥 **1C - Discuss the following questions:**

1) According to the text, what is needed to have health and happiness?

2) How does the Chinese philosophy of *yin* and *yang* explain balance?

3) Why can it be difficult to keep balance in our lives?

Part 2 - Focus on pronunciation

2A Listen to the <u>underlined</u> vowel sound in the following words. Is it pronounced /e/ or /æ/?

he<u>a</u>lthy	h<u>a</u>ppy	b<u>a</u>lance	sp<u>e</u>nd	sp<u>a</u>nned	s<u>ai</u>d	s<u>a</u>d
m<u>a</u>ny		<u>e</u>xcess	<u>a</u>ccess	we<u>a</u>lth	inst<u>ea</u>d	

Replay the recording of 2A. Pause the recording after each word.
Write the words in the correct lists below, according to the <u>underlined</u> sound.

1) Sound /e/ as in the word '*se̲nd*'	2) Sound /æ/ as in the word '*sa̲nd*'
he̲althy	*ha̲ppy*

Check your answers on page 138 before continuing.

Deletion of sounds in connected speech

In Unit 6, you learnt about the linking of words in connected speech.
In this section, you'll learn how some sounds are *deleted* in connected speech. For example:

- The sound /h/ is not always pronounced in unstressed (weak) words in connected speech.

  eg. Many books have been written about health.   / əv/
       Ask her about the book.

- The sound /d/ is often deleted in unstressed words. eg. health and happiness.

  Note: It is not necessary for learners of English to delete these sounds to be understood,
        however it is important for students to be aware of this feature of spoken language
        in order *to understand* the connected speech of native English speakers.

2B Listen to the following section of text and notice where sounds are deleted.

> Health experts suggest that to stay healthy and happy, it's important to keep our lives in
> balance. Chinese philosophy, which has spanned thousands of years, uses the principles of
> yin and yang to explain the importance of balance in life.

Note: As you have heard, the sound /h/ may be deleted in unstressed words in connected speech.
       However, the sound /h/ is generally pronounced clearly at the beginning of stressed words, such as in
       the words *healthy* and *happy*, and when following a vowel sound.

More features of connected speech

You have learnt how the pronunciation of words can vary in connected speech.
Another example of this is the pronunciation of the word 'the', which may be pronounced as /ðə/ or
/ði:/ depending on the sound which follows it. See the examples on the next page.

🦻 2C Listen to the example.

/ðə/   /ðə/   /ði:/   /ði:/
The <u>d</u>octor told th<u>e</u> <u>m</u>an th<u>e</u> <u>a</u>nswer to th<u>e</u> <u>i</u>mportant question.
/j/   /j/

Notice that '*the*' is pronounced /ðə/ before a *consonant sound* and /ði:/ before a *vowel sound.*

When 'the' is followed by a vowel sound, can you hear the linking sound /j/, pronounced as the first letter in the word '*yes*'? If not, listen to 2C again. Notice, *th<u>e</u> <u>a</u>nswer; th<u>e</u> <u>i</u>mportant*
                                                                                /j/   /j/

Part 3 - Extending the topic

Before you listen to **3A**, underline the word '*the*' in the text so that you can notice the pronunciation. As you listen:

1) Notice where '*the*' is followed by a word beginning with a consonant sound, it is pronounced /ðə/.

2) Notice where '*the*' is followed by a word beginning with a vowel sound, it is pronounced /ði:/.

Note: The word '*the*' is generally pronounced /ðə/ before words which begin with the sound /ju:/ (eg. <u>u</u>niverse).

🦻 3A Listen to the extended text on *Health and Happiness*.

Health and Happiness

Health experts suggest that to stay healthy and happy, it's important to keep our lives in balance. Chinese philosophy, which has spanned thousands of years, uses the principles of *yin* and *yang* to explain the importance of balance in life. Explained simply, *yang* represents the active elements of the universe, whereas the *yin* represents the passive elements. This expresses the importance of balance in all aspects of living. Today health experts agree that it's important to have a balanced life. For example, they've said it's necessary to have a balance between work and rest and to have a balanced exercise program. However, I'm sure you'd agree that in our busy world, it's not always easy to get and keep balance in our lives.

Due to business or study deadlines, many people work to excess; leaving little time at the end of their busy day to spend with family and friends. They eat fast-food and don't get enough rest or recreation and then suffer badly from the effects of stress. It's sad that this situation often happens when people believe that access to wealth is the answer to happiness instead of understanding the importance of balanced living.

While ambition can be a good thing, having *too much* ambition can cause a person to become 'out of balance'. Of course it's also unbalanced to spend too much time on entertainment and pleasure activities, with little or no time allocated to work or education. Balance means allocating enough time for all the important aspects of life, such as spending time with family and friends, working or studying, as well as resting and relaxing.

Experts now tell us that having balance in our life is the answer, not only to health and happiness, but also to success. If you're balanced, you'll have more energy and you'll reach your ambitions in a more relaxed fashion; with less stress. So...how balanced is *your* life? Do you need to allocate your time differently to have better balance in your life?

Note: You will see more examples of linking between vowel sounds in Part 7.

3B Extending your vocabulary

Find and underline the following words in the *last two paragraphs* of text in 3A.

allocate	ambition	relaxed	pleasure
	energy	fashion	success

Match the words you have underlined in the text with the correct meaning listed below. One has been done as an example.

1) a desire to reach a goal   *ambition*   5) share or distribute

2) power for activity   _____   6) manner, style, way

3) calm, happy   _____   7) good result, attainment

4) enjoyment, fun   _____

🦻 3B   Listen and check your answers to 3B. Repeat the words after the speaker.

Part 4 - Analysing the sounds

◀◀   Replay 3B and listen to the pronunciation of the underlined syllable in each word. (If necessary, pause the recording after each word).

Write the words in the correct columns below, then check your answers on page 138.

1) Words with the sound /e/ (as in *send*)	2) Words with the sound /æ/ (as in *sand*)
energy	*ambition* (The second syllable is stressed ie. am*bi*tion)

Part 5 - Understanding the link between spoken and written English

Spelling Lists - Ways of *spelling the sound* /e/ (as in the word *send*)

e	ea	a	other spelling
better	health	any	friend
energy	deadlines	many	

Spelling Lists - Ways of *spelling the sound* /æ/ (as in the word *sand*)

The sound /æ/ is almost always spelt with the letter 'a'. Look at the following examples.

and	fashion	balance	happiness

Part 6 - Spelling Check- Dictation

🕭 **Listen to the *Health and Happiness* text again.**

✎ **Complete the text with the correct words. (Pause the recording to write the words.)**

Health and Happiness

Health experts _____ that to stay healthy and happy, it's important to keep our lives in _____. Chinese philosophy, which has _____ thousands of years, uses the principles of *yin* and *yang* to explain the importance of balance in life. Explained simply, *yang* represents the active _____ of the universe, whereas the *yin* represents the passive elements. This _____ the importance of balance in all _____ of living. Today _____ experts agree that it's important to have a balanced life. For example, they've _____ it's necessary to have a balance between work and _____ and to have a balanced exercise program. However, I'm sure you'd agree that in our busy world, it's not always easy to _____ and keep balance in our lives.

Due to business or study deadlines, many people work to _____; leaving little time at the end of their busy day to _____ with family and _____. They eat fast-food and don't get enough rest or _____ and _____ suffer badly from the effects of _____. It's sad that this situation often happens when people believe that access to _____ is the answer to happiness _____ of understanding the importance of balanced living.

Check your answers by comparing this page with the *Health and Happiness* text in Part 1.

Part 7 - Listening Practice - More information about connected speech

Linking between vowel sounds

When a word which ends with /uː/ or /ʊ/ is followed by a word beginning with a vowel sound, speakers often link the words with the sound /w/ in fluent speech.

🕭 **7A** **Listen to the linking sound between the following words:**

Do‿it.   Who‿else?   Now‿in.

/w/   /w/   /w/

When a word which ends with /iː/ or /ɪ/, is followed by a word beginning with a vowel sound, speakers generally link the words with the sound /j/, pronounced as the first letter in the word '*yes.*

🕭 **7B** **Listen to the linking sound between the following words:**

The‿end.   We‿agree.   The‿office

/j/   / j /   /j/

Note: It is not necessary for learners of English to use these linking sounds to be understood. However, the use of these features helps the smooth flow of speech. It is also important for students to be aware of this feature of spoken language in order *to understand* the connected speech of native English speakers.

Linking between vowel sounds in conversation

🦻 **7C   Listen to the following conversation between a doctor and a patient.**

The places where the speakers link vowel sounds have been <u>underlined</u>.

✎ **Write in the linking sound /w/ or /j/ as you hear it.**
The first line has been done as an example.

Doctor: Now t<u>o a</u>nswer your question about your headaches Mrs West - I think they're th<u>e e</u>ffect
                    /w/   /j/
            of tension in your neck. Have you been feeling stressed?

Mrs West: Yes I don't seem to get time to d<u>o a</u>nything but work.

Doctor: How much time do you spend working at your desk?

Mrs West: <u>O(h) a</u>bout ten hours a day on th<u>e a</u>verage.

Doctor: Well th<u>e o</u>nl<u>y a</u>nswer is to take regular breaks or your headaches won't get better.

Mrs West: Yes <u>I e</u>xpect so.

Doctor: And I want t<u>o e</u>ncourage you t<u>o e</u>xercise regularly. Do you get much exercise?

Mrs West: No I haven't had the time or th<u>e e</u>nergy t<u>o e</u>xercise.

Doctor: Well, it's important to make th<u>e e</u>ffort t<u>o e</u>xercise. Your health is your most valuable

            asset and th<u>e o</u>nly way to prevent th<u>e e</u>ffects of stress is to be more balanced.

Mrs West: So if <u>I e</u>xercise and relax more, can <u>I e</u>xpect my headaches to g<u>o a</u>way?

Doctor: Yes and <u>I e</u>xpect th<u>e o</u>ther benefit will b<u>e i</u>ncreased energy.

Mrs West: Well I'll d<u>o e</u>verything you suggest doctor, if it'll make me feel better.

Doctor: Good. We'll get y<u>ou o</u>n an exercise program immediately!

Check your answers on page 138 before continuing.

👥 **Practise the complete conversation with a partner.**

I'll do anything you suggest doctor, if it'll make me feel better.

Good, we'll get you on an exercise program immediately!

Distinguishing between the sounds /e/ and /æ/ in fluent speech

Underline the words which are different in sentences a) and b) below.
The first one has been done as an example.

7D Listen to the sentences and tick ☑ the sentence, a) or b) that you hear.

1) ☐ a) The family was <u>said</u> to have lost everything. (said = reported)
   ☐ b) The family was <u>sad</u> to have lost everything.

2) ☐ a) The men listened to the explanation.
   ☐ b) The man listened to the explanation.

3) ☐ a) The trek was difficult and dangerous. (trek = long journey)
   ☐ b) The track was difficult and dangerous. (track = path)

4) ☐ a) The workers set out in the field. (set out = began)
   ☐ b) The workers sat out in the field.

5) ☐ a) The company had an expensive plan.
   ☐ b) The company had an expansive plan. (expansive = able to grow)

6) ☐ a) How much excess do we have? (excess = more than necessary)
   ☐ b) How much access do we have? (access = way of entrance)

7E Revision exercises – features of connected speech

◀◀ Replay the recording of 7D. Pause the recording after each sentence.
Mark where linking occurs between words ‿ in each sentence?

Remember linking generally occurs when:

❑ words ending with a <u>consonant</u> sound are followed by words starting with a <u>vowel</u> sound.

❑ words ending with a <u>consonant</u> sound are followed by words starting with the <u>same consonant sound</u>.

❑ words ending with a <u>vowel sound</u> are followed by words starting with a <u>vowel sound.</u> These words are generally linked with the sound /j/ or /w/.

Note: Linking doesn't occur where speakers pause between groups of words.

Check your answers on page 139 before continuing.

Practise pronouncing the sentences. Work with a partner.

• One person should say sentence a) or b).

• The other person should decide which sentence he/she hears.

Part 8 - Pronunciation of the letter 'c'

The letter 'c' can be pronounced as /k/ as in the word _cat_ /kæt/ or /s/ as in _city_ /sɪti:/.

8A **Listen to the following words from the _Health and Happiness_ text and decide how the letter 'c' is pronounced.**

Write the sound symbol /k/ or /s/ above the letter as in the example.

> /s/
> balanc̲e   princ̲iples   ac̲tive   importanc̲e
>
> nec̲essary   exerc̲ise   c̲ause

Check your answers on page 139 before continuing.

General rule for the pronunciation of the letter 'c '

The letter 'c' is pronounced as /s/ when followed by the letters 'i', 'e' and 'y' and is pronounced /k/ when followed by any other letter.

Note that often, in words with double 'c', such as ac̲cident, ac̲cept, ac̲cent, the first 'c' is pronounced /k/, the second is pronounced /s/. However, always check a dictionary if in doubt.

8B Practice

Using the above rule, how should the following words be pronounced?
Write /k/ or /s/ above the letter 'c' in each word to show the correct pronunciation.

A: Did you hear that C̲indy's been ac̲cepted into C̲anning C̲ollege?

B: No I didn't. She must be exc̲ited.

A: She c̲ertainly is. We're going to c̲elebrate at the C̲ity C̲ircle C̲afé. C̲an you c̲ome?

B: No I c̲an't c̲ancel my appointment at the offic̲e, but please give her my c̲ongratulations.

A: I will, of c̲ourse.

8C **Listen to the conversation.**

Did you show the correct pronunciation for 'c' in each word?
If not, look at the pronunciation rule again; then listen to the sentence again.

Check your answers on page 139.

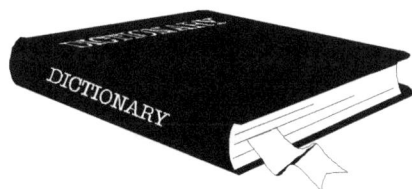

Summary - Understanding Connected Speech

When speaking in a natural, fluent, conversational way, English speakers
(including educated speakers) contract and link words to help the smooth flow of speech.

Some ways words are linked in connected speech:

1) Contracted words are linked to the word before it.

    eg.   The <u>book is</u> here.   →   The <u>book's</u> here.

             The <u>job will</u> be finished soon. → The <u>job'll</u> be finished soon.

    See Unit 2, Part 8C for more information on contractions.

2) Unstressed words are reduced (spoken quickly) For example, words like *'a', an, 'of.'*

    /ə/   /ə/

    <u>A</u> cup‿<u>of</u> tea.

    See Unit 2, Part 2 for more information on unstressed syllables.

3) Words ending with a <u>consonant</u> sound and followed by words starting with a <u>vowel</u>
   sound are usually linked.

                   →

    eg. loo<u>k</u> <u>out</u>   lookout.

    See Unit 6, Part 2 & 7 for more information on linking.

4) Words ending with a <u>consonant</u> sound are usually linked to words starting with
   the <u>same consonant sound</u>. The sound is pronounced only once, but a little longer.

                →

    eg. bu<u>s</u> <u>stop</u>   busstop

5) In fast connected speech some sounds may be deleted.
   For example, the sounds /d/ and /h/ are often deleted in unstressed words.

                  /əv/   /ən/

    eg. Many books ͪave been written about health anͩ happiness

    See Unit 7, Part 2 for more information on deletion of sounds.

6) Words ending with a <u>vowel</u> sound and words starting with a <u>vowel</u> sound can be
   linked with a linking sound like /w/ or /j/. eg. We‿only have two‿in the queue.

                                            /j/   /w/

   See Unit 7, Part 7 for more information on linking between vowel sounds.

**Understanding how words are linked in spoken English is an important step in improving
your listening skills.**

Unit 8
Medical Miracles

In this unit you will:

- Discuss the topic of Medical Miracles

- Practise distinguishing between the sounds /e/ (as in *when*) and /ɪ/ (as in *win*)

- Analyse the link between spoken and written English
  ie. ways of spelling the sounds /e/ and /ɪ/.

- Practise pronouncing consonant clusters

- Practise distinguishing between the sounds /r/ and /l/

Preliminary Listening

Listen to the vowel sounds in the following words. Can you hear the difference?

/e/ when?	/e/ bell	/e/ medal	/e/ weather
/ɪ/ win	/ɪ/ bill	/ɪ/ middle	/ɪ/ wither

Note: The sound /e/ as in when and /ɪ/ as in win, may be represented with different symbols in your dictionary, so check the words in <u>your</u> dictionary now. What symbols does your dictionary use?

Part 1 - Introduction to the topic

Think about the topic before turning the page to read and listen to the text.

The speaker will talk about *Medical Miracles*. What do you think the speaker will say?

☐ a) People now expect to <u>spend more money on medicine.</u>

or

☐ b) People now expect to <u>live longer, healthier lives</u>.

Check your answer by listening to Part 1A.

Unit 8 – Medical Miracles

In Part 1, focus on *what* the speaker says about the topic.
You will focus on *how* words are pronounced in Part 2.

1A   Listen as you read the text about *Medical Miracles*.

Medical Miracles

A miracle is an <u>incredible</u> event. In the twentieth century, many medical discoveries and <u>inventions</u> have been called 'medical miracles'. <u>Methods</u> that were considered impossible a century ago, are now regular medical practice. <u>Physical injuries</u>, which may have caused death in the past, can now be quickly fixed with <u>progressive</u> medical methods. Illnesses which, in the past, were a serious <u>threat</u> to many children can now be prevented. The lives of millions of men, women and children have been <u>extended</u> by modern medicine. People now expect to live longer, healthier lives.

Of course miracles of medicine are not <u>limited</u> only to the inventions and discoveries of the present time. Long before this century, Chinese medical books contained information on how to mix special medicines to <u>prevent</u> illness and <u>mend</u> injuries. <u>Nevertheless</u>, the medical miracles of this century have meant that millions of people have the possibility of longer, healthier and more active lives than any generation in the past. Has a specific 'medical miracle' helped you, or a friend, to live a longer, healthier and more active life?

1B Write the underlined words in the text next to the correct meaning below.
The first one has been done as an example.

1) restricted to a few   *limited*   7) repair, fix   _____

2) amazing   _____   8) a danger   _____

3) ways of doing something _____   9) modern, advanced _____

4) stop from happening _____   10) however/but   _____

5) damage to the body   _____   11) increased   _____

6) things designed, created _____

1B   Listen and check your answers to 1B. Repeat the words after the speaker.

1C   Discuss the following questions.

1) How have the medical discoveries and inventions of our generation helped people?

2) Why does the speaker say that medical miracles are not limited only to this century?

Part 2 - Focus on pronunciation

🎧 **2A** **Listen to the following words from the text.**

Which words contain the sound /e/? Which words contain the sound /ɪ/?

limited	methods	prevent	nevertheless	fixed	threat
incredible	mend	physical	injuries	extended	mix
death	women	any	friend	health	

◀◀ **Replay the recording of 2A. Pause the recording after each word.**

Write the words in the correct lists below, according to the underlined sound.

Don't be confused by the *spelling*. You need to listen to the *pronunciation* of the words!

1) Sound /e/ as in the word 'when'	2) Sound /ɪ/ as in the word 'win'
methods	*limited*

Check your answers on page 140 before continuing.

Distinguishing Syllables – revision

◀◀ **Replay Part 2A on the audio recording.**

2B Write the words in the correct columns below. One has been done as an example.

words with one syllable	words with two syllables	words with three syllables	words with four syllables
		limited	

Check your answers on page 140 before continuing.

Important Pronunciation Notes:

- The 'ed' endings on words (eg. limit<u>ed</u>) are sometimes pronounced as an extra syllable. For example, '*limited*' has three syllables, /lɪ mə təd/

  However, sometimes the 'ed' ending becomes part of the previous syllable. For example, '*fixed*' is pronounced as one syllable, /fɪkst/ not /fɪks əd/. See explanation Unit 5, Part 2.

- In many English words, two or more consonant sounds occur together within a syllable. This is called a *consonant cluster*. Sometimes a syllable is formed with a consonant cluster, as in the final syllable of the word *incredible*. See examples in Part 7B, Exercise 3.

Part 3 - Extending the topic

In Part 3, focus on *what* the speaker says about the topic.
You will focus on *how* words are pronounced in Part 4.

3A   Listen to the extended text about *Medical Miracles*.

Medical Miracles

A miracle is an incredible event. In the twentieth century, many medical discoveries and inventions have been called 'medical miracles'. Methods that were considered impossible a century ago, are now regular medical practice. Physical injuries, which may have caused death in the past, can now be quickly fixed with progressive medical methods. Illnesses which in the past, were a serious threat to many children can now be prevented. The lives of millions of men, women and children have been extended by modern medicine. People now expect to live longer, healthier lives.

Of course miracles of medicine are not limited only to the inventions and discoveries of the present time. Long before this century, Chinese medical books contained information on how to mix special medicines to prevent illness and mend injuries. Nevertheless, the medical miracles of this century have meant that millions of people have the possibility of longer, healthier and more active lives than any generation in the past. Has a specific 'medical miracle' helped you, or a friend, to live a longer, healthier and more active life?

Think about the fitting of artificial limbs which can give new mobility to accident victims. Think about the miracle of x-ray which can detect injury, and medicines which can prevent the painful symptoms of illness. Think about vaccines* which have prevented the spread of infectious disease. Think about inventions such as electronic implants which send messages to the brain to help the heart keep its regular rhythm.

New medical miracles are being discovered and invented every day. The present century promises to bring even more effective methods for treating injury and illness.

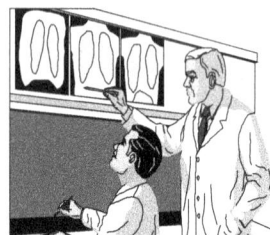

Note: *Vaccines are special medicines which prevent disease.

3B   Extending your vocabulary

Find and <u>underline</u> the following words in the last two paragraphs of text above.

limbs	victims	mobility	symptoms	detect
spread	infectious	implants	rhythm	effective

Match the words you have underlined in the text with the correct meaning listed below. One has been done as an example.

1) find, reveal   _detect_   6) increase over an area _____

2) people who are hurt   _____   7) easily infecting others_____

3) arms, legs   _____   8) having the right result_____

4) ability to move   _____   9) signs of illness   _____

5) regular beat, pulse   _____   10) electronic objects
                                               fixed into the body _____

3B Listen and check your answers to 3B. Repeat the words after the speaker.

Part 4 - Analysing the sounds

◀◀ **Replay 3B and listen to the pronunciation of the stressed syllable in each word.**
(If necessary, pause the recording after each word.)
Write the words in the correct columns below, then check your answers on page 140.

Words with the sound /e/ (as in when)	Words with the sound /ɪ/ (as in win)
detect	

Part 5 - Understanding the link between spoken and written English

Spelling Lists - Ways of *spelling the sound* /e/ (as in the word *when*)

e	ea	a	other spellings
better method	health threat	any many	friend said

Spelling Lists - Ways of *spelling the sound* /ɪ/ (as in the word *win*)

i	y	other spellings
live mix this bring	rhythm symptoms	pretty build women

Unit 8 – Medical Miracles

Part 6 - Spelling Check – Dictation

Listen to the *Medical Miracles* text again.

Complete the text with the correct words. (Pause the recording to write the words.)

Medical Miracles

A miracle is an incredible _____ . In the twentieth century, _____ medical

discoveries and inventions have been called 'medical miracles'. _____ that were

considered impossible a century ago, are now _____ medical practice. _____

injuries, which may have caused _____ in the past, can now be quickly _____ with

progressive medical methods. Illnesses _____, in the past, were a serious _____ to

_____ children can now be prevented. The lives of millions of men, _____ and

children have been extended by modern medicine. People now _____ to live longer,

_____ lives.

Part 7 - Listening Practice – Using intonation to indicate 'checking'

In Unit 5, you learnt that rising intonation is generally used by English speakers *to check or ask for further information.*

7A Listen to friends talking about medical miracles.

Can you hear where the speakers use *rising intonation* to show they are *checking or asking for further information*? Mark the rising intonation, then check your answers on page141.

A: What do you think is the most incredible medical invention?

B: You mean this century?

A: I mean ever.

B: You mean a discovery or mechanical thing?

A: It doesn't make any difference - just the most incredible thing.

B: Mm. I guess I'd have to say anesthetic. (Also spelt 'anaesthetic'.)

A: Anesthetic?

B: Mm.

A: Yeah, I guess anesthetic has made a very big impact.

B: So you agree?

A: Yes, I agree.

Note: Where two or more choices are given, intonation generally rises on the first choice/s, then falls on the final choice to show that the speaker has finished - as shown in the illustration.

You mean a discovery or mechanical thing?

... just the most incredible thing.

Consonants pronounced within one syllable – 'consonant clusters'

In many English words, two or more consonant sounds occur together within one syllable. When two or more consonant sounds are pronounced in the same syllable this is referred to as a *consonant cluster*. For example: 'fr' at the beginning of the word *friend*
'spl' at the beginning of *'splint'*.

7B   Exercise 1 - Listen to the following words and underline the consonant clusters.

bled   step   clean   please   spell   drip   slip

_____   _____   _____   _____   _____   _____   _____

_____   _____   _____   _____   _____   _____   _____

Write some one-syllable words in each list that <u>begin</u> with the <u>same</u> consonant cluster. If you are not sure of the spelling, check in your dictionary.

7B   Exercise 2 - Listen to the consonant clusters at the *end* of the following words. Underline the consonant clusters.

fist   limp   went   link   send   sing   built

_____   _____   _____   _____   _____   _____   _____

_____   _____   _____   _____   _____   _____   _____

Write one-syllable words in each list that <u>end</u> with the same consonant cluster. **Practise saying the words.**

- Take care <u>not</u> to add a vowel sound between the consonants in the words.
- Take care to pronounce the final consonant sound clearly.

Consonants pronounced as a syllable

Consonant clusters, or single consonants, are sometimes pronounced as an extra syllable. They are called syllabic consonants and are always *unstressed*.

7B   Exercise 3 - Listen to the final syllable in the following words.

able   miracle   rhythm   little

Silent letters

In English, many written words contain consonant letters that are not pronounced.

7C   Listen to the following words and draw a line through the 'silent' letter.

sign   limbs   rhythm   knee   answer   talk   island   palm   wrong

Check your answers in your dictionary or on the answer page 141.

Distinguishing between the sounds /e/ and /ɪ/ in fluent speech

Underline the words which are different in sentences a) and b) below. The first one has been done as an example.

7D Listen and tick ☑ the sentence, a) or b) that you hear.

1) ☐ a) Did you find the <u>pen</u>?
   ☐ b) Did you find the <u>pin</u>?

2) ☐ a) He put the bell on the table.
   ☐ b) He put the bill on the table.

3) ☐ a) She's become a better person.
   ☐ b) She's become a bitter person. (bitter = unhappy)

4) ☐ a) They found the medal.
   ☐ b) They found the middle.

5) ☐ a) The farmer built ten shelters for his animals in winter.
   ☐ b) The farmer built tin shelters for his animals in winter.

6) ☐ a) Could you press the left button for me, please?
   ☐ b) Could you press the lift button for me, please?

7) ☐ a) I need a desk for my computer.
   ☐ b) I need a disk for my computer.

Check your answers on page 141 before continuing.

7E   Revision

◀◀   **Replay 7D. Pause the recording after each utterance.**

Underline the stressed words and put a box around the words the speaker makes prominent.

Check your answers on page 141 before continuing.

Practise saying the sentences. Work with a partner.

• One person should say sentence a) or b).

• The other person should decide which sentence he/she hears.

Take care to pronounce the words with consonant clusters as the speaker does on the audio recording

Part 8 - Distinguishing between the sounds /r/ and /l/

🎧 **8A   Listen to the consonant sounds in contrast. Can you hear the difference?**

/r/ wrist	/r/ rims	/r/ correct ☑	/r/ wrong ☒
/l/ list	/l/ limbs	/l/ collect	/l/ long

Note: When pronouncing /r/ and /l/, the exact position of the tongue varies a little from
speaker to speaker. The following description is for general guidance only.

/r/ is made by pointing your tongue up towards (but not touching) the top of the inside of your
mouth. Use your voice.

/l/ is made by gently pressing your tongue against the ridge above your top teeth.
Use your voice.

Distinguishing between the sounds /r/ and /l/ in fluent speech

Underline the words which are different in sentences a) and b) below.

🎧 **8B   Listen and tick ☑ the sentence, a) or b), that you hear.**

1) ☐ a) Did you correct the letter?
   ☐ b) Did you collect the letter?

3) ☐ a) Show me your wrist.
   ☐ b) Show me your list.

2) ☐ a) The rims look strong.
   ☐ b) The limbs look strong.

4) ☐ a) You're going the wrong way.
   ☐ b) You're going the long way.

Check your answers on page 141 before continuing.

Practise pronouncing the sentences correctly. Work with a partner.

• One person should say sentence a) or b).

• The other person should decide which sentence he/she hear, taking turns to check
  each other's pronunciation of /r/ and /l/.

Consonant sounds

🦻 **1A** Listen to the following pairs of words. The second word has an extra consonant sound.

bell		tie		car		day	
belt		time		card		date	*January 4th*

🦻 **1B** Listen and tick ✔ the sentence, a) or b) that you hear.

1) a) ☐ I bought a bell.
   b) ☐ I bought a belt.

2) a) ☐ I want to buy a car.
   b) ☐ I want to buy a card.

3) a) ☐ Do you have the right tie?
   b) ☐ Do you have the right time?

4) a) ☐ What day is it?
   b) ☐ What date is it?

Short vowel sounds - /æ/ bat, /ɪ/ bit, /e/ bet and /ʌ/ but

🦻 **1C** Listen to the underlined vowel sounds in the following words.

Put the words in the correct column below according to the underlined sound.

		gym	jam	gem	sad	said	
built	belt	many	money	lamp	lump	limp	
	won	when	win	rest	wrist	rust	

/æ/ bat	/ɪ/ bit	/e/ bet	/ʌ/ but

🦻 **1D** Listen and tick ✔ the sentence that you hear.

1) a) ☐ The child has a lamp.
   b) ☐ The child has a limp.
   c) ☐ The child has a lump.

2) a) ☐ Did they pack everything?
   b) ☐ Did they pick everything?
   c) ☐ Did they peck everything?

3) a) ☐ There was a problem with the track
   b) ☐ There was a problem with the trick
   c) ☐ There was a problem with the trek.
   d) ☐ There was a problem with the truck.

4) a) ☐ It's batter.
   b) ☐ It's bitter.
   c) ☐ It's better.
   d) ☐ It's butter.

Unit 9
Festivals and Celebrations

In this unit you will:

• Discuss the topic of Festivals and Celebrations.

• Practise distinguishing between the sounds /e/ (as in pen) and /&/ as in (pain)

• Learn about changes in word stress patterns

• Analyse the link between spoken and written English
  ie. ways of spelling the sounds /e/ and /&/

Preliminary Listening

Note: The second sound in each pair demonstrated below is a diphthong sound /&/ (two sounds linked together).
     In diphthong sounds, the first sound is more prominent than the second sound.

Listen to the vowel sounds in the following words. Can you hear the difference?

/e/ wet	/e/ pen	/e/ sell	/e/ well
/eɪ/ weight	/eɪ/ pain	/eɪ/ sail	/eɪ/ whale

Note: The sound /e/ as in the word 'wet', and /eɪ/ as in 'weight', may be represented with different symbols in
     your dictionary, so check the words in <u>your</u> dictionary now. What symbols does your dictionary use?

Part 1 - Introduction to the topic

Think about the topic before turning the page to read and listen to the text.

The speaker will talk about *Festivals and Celebrations*. What do you think she will say?

☐ a) Festivals are celebrated mainly in Asia.

                              or

☐ b) There is a festival happening somewhere in the world almost everyday of the year.

Check your answer by listening to Part 1A.

Unit 9 – Festivals and Celebrations

In Part 1, focus on *what* the speaker says about the topic.
You will focus on *how* words are pronounced in Part 2.

1A   Listen as you read the text about *Festival and Celebrations*.

Festivals and Celebrations

Festivals and celebrations have been held since the beginning of history to celebrate special events. In ancient times, people celebrated the beginning of spring and held festivals to celebrate successful harvests. This century people celebrate for many different reasons. Some people celebrate special days to remember saints or important religious events. In some places, important leaders are hailed when national independence days are held. Celebrations are often a time when gifts are sent and family and friends get together.

In multicultural countries, where there's a mixture of different races and religions, a great variety of interesting and exciting festivals are celebrated every year. In fact, there is a festival or celebration taking place in some city in the world almost every day of the year.

1B   Write the underlined words in the text next to its correct meaning below.
The first one has been done as an example.

1) saluted, greeted, praised   *hailed*   5) of a long time ago   _____

2) things that happen   _____   6) happening   _____

3) holy people   _____   7) public celebration   _____

4) nations/people of similar
   appearance and features   _____   8) self-government, not
                                                 controlled by another   _____

1B   Listen and check your answers to 1B. Repeat the words after the speaker.

1C   Discuss the following questions

1) For what reasons have people held festivals and celebrations in the past?

2) For what reasons do people hold festivals and celebrations at the present time?

3) Can you think of examples of religious, cultural or historical celebrations which are held in your area?

Part 2 - Focus on Pronunciation

2A Listen to the words from the text. Is the underlined sound /e/ or /eɪ/?

sp<u>e</u>cial	ev<u>e</u>nts	<u>a</u>ncient	h<u>e</u>ld	h<u>ai</u>led	c<u>e</u>ntury	independ<u>e</u>nce	d<u>a</u>ys
r<u>a</u>ces	gr<u>ea</u>t	pl<u>a</u>ce	s<u>e</u>nt	s<u>ai</u>nt	c<u>e</u>lebrate	cele<u>bra</u>tion

Replay the recording of 2A. Pause the recording after each word.
Write the words in the correct columns below, according to the underlined sound.
Don't be confused by spelling. You need to listen to the *pronunciation* of the words!

1) Sound /e/ as in the word p<u>e</u>n	2) Sound /eɪ/ as in the word p<u>ai</u>n
sp<u>e</u>cial	

Check your answers on page 143 before continuing.

2B Syllables and Word Stress - Revision

Replay the recording of 2A and notice how many syllables each word contains.

Write the words in the correct columns below.
In the words with more than one syllable:
1) underline the syllable with the *main* stress,
2) write /ə/ above the unstressed, weak syllables.

> Pronunciation note:
> Words with two or more syllables will have one syllable that is stressed more than the other syllables. This is called the *main* or *primary* stress.
>
> **Some long words have *secondary* stress also. Your dictionary Pronunciation Key will show how secondary stress is indicated**
>
> **in long words listed in *your* dictionary.**

words with one syllable	words with two syllables	words with three syllables	words with four syllables

Check your answers on page 143, then practise pronouncing the words correctly.

Notice the *main* or *primary* stress is different in the words <u>ce</u>lebrate and cele<u>bra</u>tion.
When a suffix such as '*tion*' is added to a word, the *main* stress moves to the syllable immediately before the suffix.

eg. c↓elebrate   celeb↓ration

In Part 7, you will see more examples of moving word stress.

In Part 3, focus on *what* the speaker says about the topic.
You will focus on *how* words are pronounced in Part 4.

Part 3 - Extending the topic

🦻 **3A   Listen to the extended text on *Festivals and Celebrations*.**

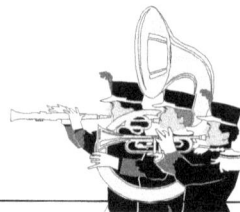

Festivals and Celebrations

Festivals and celebrations have been held since the beginning of history to celebrate special events. In ancient times, people celebrated the beginning of spring and held festivals to celebrate successful harvests. This century people celebrate for many different reasons. Some people celebrate special days to remember saints or important religious events. In some places, important leaders are hailed when national independence days are held. Celebrations are often a time when gifts are sent and family and friends get together.

In multicultural countries, where there's a mixture of different races and religions, a great variety of interesting and exciting festivals are celebrated every year. In fact, there is a festival or celebration taking place in some city in the world almost every day of the year.

In some celebrations, people wear their national dress, decorate their homes and public places and play special games. Many festivals involve parades where people are entertained by people dressed as animals to tell special tales or legends. Religious celebrations are often a time to pray and remember past events.

When celebrating special events, people around the world use different ways to measure the time in a year when the special day will be remembered. In other words, they use different calendars to mark special events. For example, the Hindu and Muslim calendars are based on the phases of the Moon, whereas the calendar used mainly in western society (known as the Gregorian calendar), is based on the timing of the earth's journey around the Sun. As a result, many people today use the Gregorian calendar for business and day to day living, but use their religious calendar to mark the special dates of festivals and religious celebrations.

3B Extending your vocabulary

Find and <u>underline</u> the following words in the last two paragraphs of text in 3A.

dr<u>e</u>ss	*d<u>e</u>cor<u>a</u>te	games	m<u>a</u>ny	par<u>a</u>des	*<u>e</u>ntert<u>ai</u>ned
t<u>a</u>les	l<u>e</u>gends	pr<u>ay</u>	m<u>ea</u>sure	b<u>a</u>sed (on)	ph<u>a</u>ses

* Pronunciation note: The words *decorate* and *entertained* contain both sounds /e/ and /eɪ/

eg. d<u>e</u>cor<u>a</u>te   <u>e</u>ntert<u>ai</u>ned
    /e/ /eɪ/   /e/   /eɪ/

Match the words you have underlined in the text with the correct meaning listed below. One has been done as an example.

1) make more attractive/beautiful   _decorate_   7) clothing   _____

2) amused/pleased   _____   8) interesting stories   _____

3) activities played for fun   _____   9) established on   _____

4) to request or thank God   _____   10) calculate   _____

5) periods of time in the
   development of something   _____   11) a lot of   _____

6) historical stories
   (which may not be true)   _____   12) public processions _____

3B   Listen and check your answers to 3B. Repeat the words after the speaker.

Part 4 - Analysing the sounds

Replay 3B and listen to the pronunciation of the underlined syllable in each word.
(If necessary, pause the recording after each word.)
Write the words in the correct columns below, then check your answers on page 143.

1) Words with the sound /e/ as in _pen_	2) Words with the sound /eɪ/ as in _pain_
d_e_corate	enter_tai_ned

Part 5 - Understanding the link between spoken and written English

Spelling Lists - Ways of _spelling the sound_ /e/ (as in the word r_e_d)

e	ea	a	other spelling
h_e_ld	m_ea_sure	_a_ny	s_ai_d
sp_e_cial	w_ea_ther	m_a_ny	

Spelling Lists - Ways of _spelling the sound_ /eɪ/ (as in the word d_ay_)

a...e	ay	ai	ei	ea
pl_a_ce	d_ay_	w_ai_t	_ei_ght	gr_ea_t
par_a_de	alw_ay_s	compl_ai_n	w_ei_ght	br_ea_k

Unit 9 – Festivals and Celebrations

Part 6 - Spelling Check- Dictation

Listen to the *Festivals and Celebrations* text again.

Complete the text with the correct words. (Pause the recording to write the words.)

Festivals and Celebrations

Festivals and celebrations have been _____ since the beginning of history to celebrate _____ events. In ancient times, people celebrated the beginning of spring and held festivals to celebrate successful harvests. This century people celebrate for _____ different reasons. Some people celebrate special _____ to remember saints or important religious events. In some _____, important leaders are _____ when national independence days are _____. Celebrations are often a time when gifts are _____ and family and _____ get together.

In multicultural countries, where there's a mixture of different _____ and religions, a _____ variety of interesting and exciting festivals are celebrated every year. In fact, there is a festival or celebration taking place in some city in the world almost every day of the year.

Part 7 - Listening Practice

7A Listen to someone asking questions about cultural celebrations.

Complete the questions as you listen. (Pause the recording while you write.)

1) _____ popular cultural celebration?

2) _____ celebrate it?

3) _____ celebrate it?

4) _____ celebrating it?

Check your answers on page 143 before continuing.

7B Review - Features of spoken English

◄◄ **Replay the recording of 7A. Pause the recording after each sentence.**
   Which words are difficult to hear because they're unstressed or reduced?

1) Write a schwa symbol /ə/ above the unstressed, reduced words.
2) Underline the words with stressed syllables in each question.
3) Draw a box around the words that the speakers make most prominent.

Check your answers on page 144, then practise asking the questions.

Moving word stress

In spoken English, the *main* or *primary* stress in a word sometimes moves when the function of the word changes; for example, when a verb, <u>ce</u>lebrate changes to a noun, '*cele<u>bra</u>tion*'.

7C Listen to the following words, and underline the syllable which has the *main* stress.

The first one has been done as an example.

verb	noun
eg. <u>ce</u>lebrate	cele<u>bra</u>tion
educate	education
examine	examination
communicate	communication

Note: In words ending 'ion', the main word stress is on the syllable *before* the suffix 'ion'.

7D The following words refer to places or nationalities. Complete the table below by writing the words in the correct column. Some have been done as examples.

Japan	Italian	China	Portugal	Chinese
Tonga	Egypt	Japanese	Italy	
Canada	Egyptian	Canadian	Portuguese	Tongan

Country	Nationality	Country	Nationality
1) *Japan* ——→	*Japanese*	5) ——→	*Chinese*
2) *Egypt* ——→		6) ——→	*Portuguese*
3) ——→	*Italian*	7) *Tonga* ——→	
Canada ——→			

7E Listen and check your answers.

The speaker will say the country and then the nationality.
<u>Underline</u> the stressed syllables in each word as you listen.

Check your answers on page 144.

More about moving word stress:

In 7C you learnt that primary word stress may move as the function of a word changes. Another example of this is when nouns (*names of places/things*) become adjectives (*describing someone/something*).

For example, in the noun, Ja<u>pan</u>, the *second* syllable has the main stress.
However, in the adjective Japa<u>ne</u>se, the *third* syllable has the main stress.

Note: Moving stress patterns do not apply in every case.
For example, in '<u>To</u>nga' and '<u>To</u>ngan', the stress is on the *same* syllable in both words.

Remember: Your dictionary will show how to pronounce word stress correctly.
If necessary, revise *Using Your Dictionary* in Unit 3, Part 2C.

Distinguishing between the sounds /e/ and /eɪ/ in fluent speech

Underline the words which are different in sentences a) and b) below.
The first one has been done as an example.

7F   Listen and tick ☑ the sentence, a) or b), that you hear.

1) ☐ a) It's better not to make the children <u>wet</u>.
    ☐ b) It's better not to make the children <u>wait</u>.

2) ☐ a) Where's the pen.
    ☐ b) Where's the pain.

3) ☐ a) Where did you sell the boat?
    ☐ b) Where did you sail the boat?

4) ☐ a) Did he tell you about the debt? (debt = money owed)
    ☐ b) Did he tell you about the date?

5) ☐ a) We saw the well near the rocks.
    ☐ b) We saw the whale near the rocks.

6) ☐ a) He tested each variety of wine.
    ☐ b) He tasted each variety of wine.

7) ☐ a) It's too hot here. Let's stand in the shed.
    ☐ b) It's too hot here. Let's stand in the shade.

8) ☐ a) Could you put some pepper on the table please. (pepper = spice added to food)
    ☐ b) Could you put some paper on the table please.

Check your answers on page 144.

7G   Revision exercises

**Replay the recording of 7F. Pause the recording after each sentence.
Underline the stressed words in each sentence.
Draw a [box] around the words that the speakers make most prominent.**

Note: In sentence 6) above, the speaker puts equal stress on each content word, therefore no word is made more prominent than the others.

Check your answers on page 144.

Practise pronouncing the sentences correctly. Work with a partner.

• One person should say sentence a) or b).

• The other person should decide which sentence he/she hears.

Part 8 - Sounds /f/ and /v/

The sounds /f/ and /v/ are sometimes confused by learners of English.

8A Listen to the consonant sounds in contrast. Can you hear the difference?

/f/ few	/f/ fan	/f/ fast	/f/ fines
/v/ view	/v/ van	/v/ vast	/v/ vines

- /f/ is made by placing your top teeth on your lower lip. Gently blow air out between your teeth and lip. Don't use your voice. /f/ is a voiceless consonant sound.

- /v/ is made by placing your top teeth on your lower lip. Use your voice box to make the sound /v/.

8B Listen and repeat the following words from the *Festivals and Celebrations* text.

festival   gifts   harvests   events   every   variety   different

Distinguishing between the sounds /f/ and /v/ in fluent speech

Underline the words that are different in sentences a) and b) below.
The first one has been done as an example.

8C Listen and tick ✔ the sentence, a) or b), that you hear.

1) ☐ a) They had a <u>few</u> of the games at their house.
    ☐ b) They had a <u>view</u> of the games at their house.

2) ☐ a) The fan isn't working properly.
    ☐ b) The van isn't working properly.

3) ☐ a) The ocean liner is fast and comfortable for passengers.
    ☐ b) The ocean liner is fast and comfortable for passengers.

4) ☐ a) The fines are much higher than last year.
    ☐ b) The vines are much higher than last year.

Check your answers on page 144.

Practise pronouncing the sentences correctly. Work with a partner.

- One person should say sentence a) or b).

- The other person should decide which sentence he/she hears.

Unit 10
Time and Change

- Is your life very different to that of your grandparents?

- What are the main changes that have happened?

- Is life better now than it was ninety years ago?

In this unit you will:

- Discuss the topic of 'Time and Change'

- Distinguish between the sounds /aɪ/ as in 'why' and /eɪ/ as in 'way'.

- Practise pronouncing these sounds correctly in fluent speech.

- Analyse the different ways of spelling these sounds
  ie. ways of spelling the sounds /aɪ/ and /eɪ/

- Revise linking, contractions, and sound deletion in connected speech.

Preliminary Listening

Note: The following sounds comprise two vowel sounds linked together, known as '*diphthongs*'.
Notice that the first sound in each diphthong is more prominent than the second sound.

Listen to the vowel sounds in the following words. Can you hear the difference?

/aɪ/ why	/aɪ/ pine	/aɪ/ high	/aɪ/ buy
/eɪ/ way	/eɪ/ pain	/eɪ/ hay	/eɪ/ bay

Note: The sound /aɪ/ as in the word 'why' and /eɪ/ as in 'way', may be represented with different symbols in your dictionary, so check the words in <u>your</u> dictionary now. What symbols does your dictionary use?

Part 1 - Introduction to the topic

Think about the topic before turning the page to read and listen to the text.

The speaker will talk about *Time and Change*. What do you think the speaker will say?

☐ a) The pace of life hasn't changed much in the last five years.

or

☐ b) It's impossible to deny that life has changed in many ways.

Check your answer by listening to Part 1A.

In Part 1, focus on *what* the speaker says about the topic.
You will focus on *how* words are pronounced in Part 2.

1A   Listen as you read the text about *Time and Change*.

Time and Change

It's right to say that life has changed. The <u>pace</u> and <u>style</u> of life today is not the same as it was in our grandparent's day. Science has changed the way of life in almost every place on earth at quite an amazing pace. I'm sure you can <u>relate</u> many changes that have <u>taken place</u> in your lifetime.

We now have machines that reduce work and make more free time available each day. We've <u>gained</u> better ways to fight <u>crime</u> and to take away pain. We can now travel great distances at an <u>amazingly</u> fast pace by plane or train, where people of the past had to allow a lot of time to <u>hike</u>, ride or sail to far away places. We can now communicate <u>instantaneously</u> by <u>e-mail</u> rather than waiting many days to receive letters by regular mail. Yes - it's impossible to <u>deny</u> that the pace and style of life has changed in many ways!

1B   Write the underlined words in the text next to the correct meaning below. The first one has been done as an example.

1) speed of progress   *pace*   7) instantly, immediately   _____

2) tell, talk about   _____   8) surprisingly   _____

3) type, kind of   _____   9) walk a long way   _____

4) obtained/achieved   _____   10) say it is not true   _____

5) happened, occurred   _____   11) bad, illegal action   _____

6) electronic mail   _____

1B   Listen and check your answers to 1B. Repeat the words after the speaker.

1C   Now discuss the following questions:

1)   Why has life changed since our grandparent's day?

2)   What examples does the text give of ways that life has changed?

Part 2 - Focus on Pronunciation

🦻 **2A** **Listen to the underlined vowel sound in the following words.**

Which words contain the sound /aɪ/? Which contain the sound /eɪ/?

r<u>i</u>ght	s<u>ay</u>	l<u>i</u>fe	p<u>a</u>ce	st<u>y</u>le	s<u>a</u>me	pl<u>a</u>ce
m<u>ai</u>l	g<u>ai</u>ned	t<u>i</u>me	cr<u>i</u>me	h<u>i</u>ke	s<u>ai</u>l	den<u>y</u>

◄◄ **Replay 2A. Pause the recording after each word.**
Write the words in the correct lists below, according to the underlined sound.
Don't be confused by the spelling. You need to listen to the *pronunciation* of the words!

1) Sound /aɪ/ as in the word '*why*'	2) Sound /eɪ/ as in the word '*way*'
right	*say*

Check your answers on page 145 before continuing.

🦻 **2B** **Listen to the questions.**

✏️ **Mark where sounds are deleted to form contractions.**

1) How has communication changed in the last twenty-five years?

2) How has transportation changed in the last twenty-five years?

3) How has education changed in the last twenty-five years?

4) How has entertainment changed in the last twenty-five years?

5) What changes have taken place in your life the last five years?

6) How do you think science will change our lives in the next five years?

👤 **Check the answers on page 145 before you practise reading the questions aloud.**

Unit 10 – Time and Change

In Part 3, focus on *what* the speaker says about the topic.
You will focus on *how* words are pronounced in Part 4.

Part 3 - Extending the topic

👂 **3A   Listen to the extended text on *'Time and Change'*.**

Time and Change

It's right to say that life has changed. The pace and style of life today is not the same as it was in our grandparent's day. Science has changed the way of life in almost every place on earth at quite an amazing pace. I'm sure you can relate many changes that have taken place in your lifetime.

We now have machines that reduce work and make more free time available each day. We've gained better ways to fight crime and to take away pain. We can now travel great distances at an amazingly fast pace by plane or train, where people of the past had to allow a lot of time to hike, ride or sail to far away places. We can now communicate instantaneously by e-mail rather than waiting many days to receive letters by regular mail. Yes - it's impossible to deny that the pace and style of life has changed in many ways!

But people manage change in different ways. Some people happily embrace change; for them change is exciting. They're impatient for the latest 'high-tech' devices to go on sale. In fact, their greatest aim is to buy the latest styles and designs as soon as they're available.

Other people, however, complain: 'I can't keep pace with all this change; it drives me crazy! I'm always in a race with time!' Then there are other people who may even find change a little frightening. These people sigh and say: 'Why can't things just stay the same?'

Well, despite our feelings about change, can we really do anything to stop change? Listen to the following advice about life and change and decide for yourself if you think it's wise.

Life is change
So don't be afraid and don't try to fight it.
Just try to make your life as you'd really like it.

3B   Extending your vocabulary

✏️   **Find and underline the following words in the last four paragraphs of text above.**

embrace	impatient	latest	'high – tech'	devices	drives me crazy
wise	frightening	sigh	despite	advice	

Match the words you have <u>underlined</u> in the text with the correct meaning listed below.
One has been done as an example.

1) advanced technology   *high-tech*   7) mechanical things   _____

2) accept, welcome   _____   8) worrying, alarming   _____

3) most recent   _____   9) regardless of   _____

4) suggestion   _____   10) not happy to wait   _____

5) makes me angry/upset   _____   11) make a sound which
                                                     expresses unhappiness _____

6) sensible   _____

3B   Listen and check your answers to 3B. Repeat the words after the speaker.

Part 4 - Analysing the sounds

4A   Listen to the following words from the text.

Write the words in the columns below, according to the stressed sound.
(Pause the recording after each word so you can write the answer.)

| embr<u>a</u>ce | <u>la</u>test | dr<u>i</u>ves | <u>cra</u>zy | sale | style | I'm | aim |
| wise | ways | de<u>vi</u>ces | des<u>pi</u>te | ad<u>vi</u>ce | sigh | say |

1) Words with the sound /aɪ/ (as in *why*)	2) Words with the sound /eɪ/ (as in *way*)
	embr<u>a</u>ce

4B   Look at the illustration on title page for this unit.

Some of the items illustrated are pronounced with the sounds /aɪ/ or /eɪ/.

Write the names of three items shown in the illustration in each of the lists above.

Check your answers on page 145 before continuing.

Part 5 - Understanding the link between spoken and written English

Spelling Lists - Ways of *spelling the sound* /aɪ/ (as in the word *why*)

i...e*	y	i + gh	other
time	why	fight	eye
life	try	sigh	buy
advice	deny	might	

Spelling Lists - Ways of *spelling the sound* /eɪ/ (as in the word *way*)

a...e*	ay	ai	ei	other
same	say	sail	reins	they
place	day	mail	weight	obey
change	way	wait		

Spelling and Pronunciation Guidelines

🦻 **5A** **Listen to following words.**

kit   kite

hat   hate

Can you see the pronunciation pattern?

The following rule is useful for many words of one syllable:

'The letter 'e' at the end of a word (often) makes the first vowel sound as its alphabet name.'

Complete the tables on the right:

🦻 **5B** **Check your answers as you listen to the way the pronunciation of the words can change with the addition of a final letter 'e'.**

letter	sound /ɪ/ becomes	sound /aɪ/
i	kit ⟶	kite
	hid	
	pin	
	bit	
	quit	

letter	sound /æ/ becomes	sound /eɪ/
a	hat ⟶	hate
	cap	
	rat	
	tap	
	mat	

Note: There are exceptions to the above rule. For example, the words 'give' /gɪv/ and 'have' /hæv/ are pronounced with a short vowel sound.

Part 6 - Spelling Check- Dictation

👂 **Listen to the text about *Time and Change* again.**

✏️ **Complete the text with the correct words.** (Pause the recording to write the words.)

Time and Change

It's _____ to say that life has changed. The _____ and _____ of life today is not
the _____ as it was in our grandparent's day. Science has _____ the way of life
in almost every _____ on earth at _____ an amazing pace. I'm sure you can
relate many changes that have _____ place in your lifetime.

We now have machines that reduce work and _____ more free time available each day.
We've _____better ways to fight _____and to take away _____. We can now
travel great distances at an amazingly fast pace by _____ or _____, where people
of the past had to allow a lot of _____ to hike, ride or _____ to far away places. We
can now communicate instantaneously by e-mail rather than waiting many _____ to
receive letters by regular _____. Yes - it's impossible to deny that the pace and
_____ of life has changed in many _____!

Check your answers by comparing this page with the *Time and Change* text (Part 1A).

Part 7 - Listening Practice

👂 **7A** **Listen to a conversation between friends, Mike and Kay, about time and change.**

✏️ **Complete the conversation, writing contractions as you hear them.**

Mike: _____since I was a child. _____pace of life these days.

Kay: Why do you say that? _____ great these days.

Mike: _____racing with time. _____changes.

Kay: But _____change, _____very exciting!

Mike: Mm_____ probably right. But it drives me crazy just the same.

Contractions are used more in speaking than writing, but they are often used in writing that shows conversation..

**7B - Check your answers on page 146 before you practise the conversation with a partner.
Do you agree with Mike or Kay's opinion about change?**

Distinguishing between sounds /aɪ/ and /eɪ/ in fluent speech

Underline the words which are different in sentences a) and b) below. The first one has been done as an example.

7C Listen and tick ☑ the sentence, a) or b) that you hear.

1) ☐ a) Where's the <u>pine</u>?
   ☐ b) Where's the <u>pain</u>?

2) ☐ a) I'm going to have a light lunch today. (light lunch = small lunch)
   ☐ b) I'm going to have a late lunch today.

3) ☐ a) Did he finish his rice?
   ☐ b) Did he finish his race?

4) ☐ a) The plane's lighter than last time. (lighter = not as heavy)
   ☐ b) The plane's later than last time.

5) ☐ a) Could you type the lecture for me, please?
   ☐ b) Could you tape the lecture for me, please? (tape = record)

6) ☐ a) It's important to give the right prize to the winner. (prize = reward)
   ☐ b) It's important to give the right praise to the winner. (praise = words of approval)

7) ☐ a) I'm to finish the report by Friday.
   ☐ b) Aim to finish the report by Friday.

Check your answers on page 146 before continuing.

7D Revision exercise – hearing the prominent words

◄◄ **Replay Part 7C on the audio recording. Pause the recording after each sentence. Draw a box around the word/s the speaker makes *most* prominent in each utterance.**

Now practise pronouncing the sentences. Work with a partner.

- One person should say sentence a) or b).

- The other person should decide which sentence he/she hears.

Part 8 - Pronunciation of the letter 'g'

The letter 'g' can be pronounced as /g/ as in the word '*game*' /geɪm/.
The letter 'g' can be pronounced as /dʒ/ as in the word '*page*' /peɪdʒ/.
The letter 'g' is usually silent when followed by /h/ as in '*sight*' /saɪt/.

General rule for the pronunciation of the letter 'g'

- The letter 'g' is pronounced as /dʒ/ when followed by the letters 'i', 'e' and 'y'.
- The letter 'g' is pronounced as /g/ when followed by any other letter, except when it is followed by /h/ which makes it 'silent'.

Using the above rule, decide how the following words should be pronounced before you listen to the answers?

gained	change	begin	sigh	great	regular
manage	weight	high	game	gem	

Using the rule above, write the words in the correct column below.
Then listen to the answers given in 8A.

1) /g/ as in the word 'game'	2) silent /g/	3) /dʒ/ as in the word 'page'

🦻 8A   **Listen and check your answers. Repeat the words after the speaker**.
   Note: The speaker will give the answers for each list above, 1), 2) and 3).

Unit 11

The World of Sport

- Can you name the sport illustrated in each box?

- Which sport is popular in your area?

- Which have you tried?

- Which would you like to try?

- What other types of sport are played in your area?

In this unit you will:

- Discuss the topic of Sport.

- Practise distinguishing between the sound /ɜ:/ in '<u>wor</u>ld' and /ɔ:/ in '<u>spor</u>t'.

- Practise pronouncing the sounds /ɜ:/ and /ɔ:/ in fluent speech

- Analyse the link between spoken and written English
  ie. ways of spelling the sounds /ɜ:/ and /ɔ:/.

- Examine and practise the pronunciation of 's' and 'es' endings on words.

- Analyse some ways English speakers use pausing and intonation in conversation

Preliminary Listening

🎧 **Listen to the vowel sounds in the following words. Can you hear the difference?**

/ɜ:/ learn	/ɜ:/ curl	/ɜ:/ work	/ɜ:/ bird
/ɔ:/ lawn	/ɔ:/ call	/ɔ:/ walk	/ɔ:/ board

Note: The sound /ɜ:/ as in the word '*work*', and /ɔ:/ as in '*walk*', may be represented with different symbols in your dictionary, so check the words in <u>your</u> dictionary now. What symbols does your dictionary use?

Part 1 - Introduction to the topic

Think about the topic before turning the page to read and listen to the text.

The speaker will talk about *The World of Sport.* What do you think the speaker will say?

☐ a) Most sports reporters suggest that sport generally has a <u>positive</u> effect on people.

or

☐ b) Most sports reporters suggest that sport generally has a <u>negative</u> effect on people.

Check your answer by listening to Part 1A.

In Part 1, focus on *what* the speaker says about the topic.
You will focus on *how* words are pronounced in Part 2.

1A Listen as you read the text about *The World of Sport*.

The World of Sport

What's the difference between a hobby and a sport? A hobby is an activity or interest that people choose and learn for relaxation or fun. A sport can also be a hobby, however, sport usually involves skill or training. Sport usually involves some <u>sort</u> of contest and often a lot of <u>firm</u> rules. Sport involves people trying to <u>perform</u> better than their competitors; trying to be first or trying to record better <u>scores</u> than before. And of course, for the person who wants to win an <u>award</u>, sport can involve a lot of hard work.

In recent years, there has been talk about the general effects of sport. Questions have been asked about whether sport generally has a positive or negative effect on competitors and <u>audiences</u>. Some reporters have suggested that sport is not played but <u>fought</u> on the field or <u>court</u>, and therefore suggested that children should not be <u>forced</u> to learn sport at school. Most reporters, however, suggest that generally sport has a positive effect, as the purpose of all sport is to <u>form</u> friendship and honest competition.
What's your opinion? <u>In a word</u>, do you think the effect of sport is generally positive or negative?

1B Write the <u>underlined</u> words in the text next to the correct meaning below. The first one has been done as an example.

1) in summary, briefly   *(in) a word*   6) strict/definite   _____

2) an area for playing games _____   7) to make/ build   _____

3) compelled, with no choice _____   8) type/variety   _____

4) points won in a game   _____   9) do/act   _____

5) people who watch or listen _____   10) prize or payment   _____

                                                  11) past form of 'fight' _____

1B Listen and check your answers to 1B. Repeat the words after the speaker.

1C Discuss the following questions.

1) How is sport different to a hobby?

2) Why do most sports reporters think sport has a positive effect?

Part 2 - Focus on Pronunciation

2A Listen to the following words from the text.

Notice the underlined vowel sound. Is it the sound /ɜː/ or sound /ɔː/?

Don't be confused by the *spelling*. You need to listen to the *pronunciation* of the words!

f<u>ir</u>m	f<u>or</u>m	l<u>ear</u>n	c<u>our</u>t	s<u>or</u>t	f<u>ir</u>st	f<u>or</u>ced
a w<u>or</u>d	aw<u>ar</u>d	<u>au</u>diences	w<u>or</u>k	sc<u>or</u>es	f<u>ou</u>ght	

Replay the recording of 2A. Pause the recording after each word.
Write the words in the correct lists below, according to the <u>underlined</u> sound.

1) Sound /ɜː/ as in the word 'work'	2) Sound /ɔː/ as in the word 'walk'
firm	form

Check your answers on page 147 before continuing.

Pronunciation of words ending with 's' or 'es'

The 's' or 'es' endings on words (nouns or verbs) may be pronounced as an extra syllable.
For example, 'causes' has two syllables /kɔːz əz/; 'audiences' has four syllables /ɔːdiːən s<u>əz</u>/.

However, sometimes the 'es' ending becomes part of the syllable before it.
For example, 'scores' is pronounced as one syllable, /skɔːz/.

The pronunciation used depends on the sound that precedes the final 's' or 'es'.

2B Listen to the 's' ending in the following words. Repeat the words after the speaker.

'es' pronounced as an extra syllable - /əz/ or /ɪz/	2) 's' or 'es' as part of the preceding syllable - pronounced /z/	3) 's' or 'es' as part of the preceding syllable - pronounced /s/
mi<u>sses</u> fini<u>shes</u> wat<u>ches</u> ju<u>dges</u>	w<u>ar</u>s /wɔːz/ /z/ follows all vowel <u>sounds</u> bal<u>ls</u> ser<u>ves</u>	ma<u>kes</u> ge<u>ts</u> ma<u>ps</u> lau<u>ghs</u> /laːfs/
The sound /əz/ follows sounds: /s/ /z/ /ʃ/ spelt 'sh', /tʃ/ spelt 'ch' and sound /dʒ/, usually spelt 'g'.	The sound /z/ follows all vowel sounds and sounds /b/ /d/ /g/ /l/ /m/ /n/ /r/ /v/	The sound /s/ follows sounds: /k/ /t/ /p/ /f/

2C Listen and add the following words to the correct column above. (Answers p. 147)

games	races	rules	stars	catches	looks	bats

Unit 11 – The World of Sport

In Part 3, focus on *what* the speaker says about the topic.
You will focus on *how* words are pronounced in Part 4.

Part 3 - Extending the topic

🦻 **3A   Listen to the extended text on the *World of Sport*.**

The World of Sport

What's the difference between a hobby and a sport? A hobby is an activity or interest that people choose and learn for relaxation or fun. A sport can also be a hobby, however, sport usually involves skill or training. Sport usually involves some sort of contest and often a lot of firm rules. Sport involves people trying to perform better than their competitors; trying to be first or trying to record better scores than before. And of course, for the person who wants to win an award, sport can involve a lot of hard work.

In recent years, there has been talk about the general effects of sport. Questions have been asked about whether sport generally has a positive or negative effect on competitors and audiences. Some reporters have suggested that sport is not played but fought on the field or court, and therefore suggested that children should not be forced to learn sport at school. Most reporters, however, suggest that generally sport has a positive effect, as the purpose of all sport is to form friendship and honest competition.

What's your opinion? In a word, do you think the effect of sport is generally positive or negative?

The Olympic Games are certainly a good example of 'world sport' as they are organised every four years for competitors from all over the world. The idea behind the modern Olympic Games, as suggested in the Olympic Oath[1], is to further 'the true spirit of sportsmanship, for the glory of sport and the honour of our teams'.

The Olympic Creed[2] suggests the important thing is not to have won, but 'to have fought well'. Although this suggests that sport is like war, what it really means is that being involved is more important than winning.

What do you think? Do the Olympic Games serve a worthy purpose?

3B Extending your vocabulary
Find and <u>underline</u> the following words in the last three paragraphs of the text above.

certainly	organised	further	sportsmanship	glory
	worthy	serve	purpose	

---

[1] The Olympic Oath, written by Baron de Coubertin, is spoken by an athlete from the host nation on behalf of all the Olympic competitors.
[2] The Olympic Creed (set of beliefs) was adopted by Baron de Coubertin in 1908.

Match the words you have underlined in the text with the correct meaning listed below. has been done as an example.

1) fair, honest competition   _sportsmanship_

2) excellence/greatness   _____

3) promote, advance   _____

4) help, assist   _____

5) good, respectable   _____

6) aim, intended result_____

7) definitely   _____

8) arranged   _____

Check your answers on page 147 before continuing.

3B   Listen and check your answers to 3B. Repeat the words after the speaker.

Part 4 - Analysing the sounds

Replay 3B and listen to the pronunciation of the stressed syllable in each word.
(If necessary, pause the recording after each word).
Write the words in the correct columns below, then check your answers on page 147.

1) Words with the sound /ɜː/ as in _world_	2) Words with the sound /ɔː/ as in _sport_
	sportsmanship

Part 5 - Understanding the link between spoken and written English

Spelling Lists - Ways of _spelling_ the sound /ɜː/ as in the word _world_

ir	er	or	ur	ear
b<u>ir</u>d	c<u>er</u>tain	w<u>or</u>d	t<u>ur</u>n	l<u>ear</u>n
f<u>ir</u>st	h<u>er</u>	w<u>or</u>k	f<u>ur</u>ther	<u>ear</u>ly

Note:
The letter 'r' after the vowel letters in the words above, is pronounced clearly in some varieties of English; notably, American and Scottish. In other varieties of English, 'r' isn't pronounced in the above words. These differences do _not_ cause problems in communication.

In <u>all</u> varieties of English, 'r' is generally pronounced when followed by a vowel sound. For example, in _the word o<u>r</u>ange_, the 'r' is pronounced in _all varieties of English_ as a vowel sound _follows_ the 'r'.

Spelling Lists - Ways of _spelling_ the sound /ɔː/ as in the word _sport_

or	a	au	ou	aw
sp<u>or</u>t	<u>a</u>ll	<u>au</u>dience	c<u>our</u>t	s<u>aw</u>
f<u>or</u>m	w<u>a</u>r	c<u>au</u>ght	f<u>ou</u>ght	l<u>aw</u>

Part 6 - Spelling Check-Dictation

🦻 **Listen to the text about _The World of Sport_ again.**

✎ **Complete the text with the correct words.** (Pause the recording to write the word.)

The World of Sport

What's the difference between a hobby and a sport? A hobby is an activity or interest that people choose and _____ for relaxation or fun. A sport can also be a hobby, however, sport usually involves skill or training. Sport usually involves some _____ of contest and often a lot of _____ rules. Sport involves people trying to _____ better than their competitors; trying to be _____ or trying to record better _____ than before. And of course, for the _____ who wants to win an _____, sport can involve a lot of hard _____.

In recent years, there has been _____ about the general effects of sport. Questions have been asked about whether sport generally has a positive or negative effect on competitors and _____. Some reporters have suggested that sport is not played but _____ on the field or _____, and therefore suggested that children should not be _____ to learn sport at school. Most reporters, however, suggest that generally sport has a positive effect, as the _____ of all sport is to _____ friendship and honest competition.

Part 7 - Listening Practice – Pausing and Intonation

In questions where two or more choices or alternatives are given, speakers use pausing and intonation to make the important parts of the message more prominent. Intonation generally rises on the first alternative/s, then falls on the final alternative to show that the speaker has finished.

In the following examples, notice how the speakers use pausing and intonation to make the important information more prominent.

🦻 **7A   Listen to the examples:**

(Words with stressed syllables are <u>underlined</u>. Prominent words are in a box.)

Do you pre<u>fer</u> tennis, cricket or volley <u>ball</u>?

Do you <u>think</u> the e<u>ffect</u> of <u>sport</u> is positive or negative?

🦻 **7B   Listen to the following questions. Mark the intonation as you listen.**

Do you pre<u>fer</u> playing or watching <u>sport</u>?

Do you pre<u>fer</u> indoor or outdoor <u>sport</u>?

Do you pre<u>fer</u> individual or team <u>sport</u>?

Check your answers on page 148 then practise asking the questions.

When saying lists of numbers, such as phone numbers or account numbers, speakers make understanding easier by dividing a long list of numbers into smaller groups of numbers, pausing at the end of each group. They use falling intonation to indicate the final number.

🦻 **7C** **Listen to the example.**   549   672   464

- Can you hear the pause at the end of each group of numbers?

- Can you hear the falling intonation on the last number showing that the speaker has finished?

> Note: Not <u>all</u> speakers use rising intonation between groups of numbers as in the example. However, generally speakers finish with falling intonation to indicate the last number.

Practise saying *your* **phone number (or another number) with pausing after each group of three or four numbers. Remember to use falling intonation to indicate the last number.**

In conversation, speakers pause to make information prominent; especially when listing items or saying long numbers. You will hear examples of this in the following conversation.

After completing the conversation below, you will examine where the speakers pause to make important information prominent.

🦻 **7D** **Listen to the conversation between friends at work.**

✎ Pause the recording to write the missing words.

Ann: Look what I've just bought at the _____ store - some _____, some _____, four soccer balls, a drawing board, some golf _____ and some assorted ball games.

Bob: It looks like you've bought the whole _____.

Ann: I know, but there's _____. I've also ordered _____ surfboards.

Bob: Four surfboards? *What on earth for?

Ann: For birthday presents for Paul and Dawn and my _____. All their birthdays are in _____ so it's perfect. And everything in the store was forty percent off the normal price.

Bob: _____ percent? That's a bargain. I should call into the store after _____.

Ann: I think it closes at _____ and the sale finishes tomorrow morning. Why don't you give them a _____?

Bob: OK. Do you know the number?

Ann: Yes I have it here. It's _____.

Bob: _____. I'll call them now.
        I could use a new _____ and some new shirts.

*'What on earth for?' is an expression used when asking the reason *why* someone has done a surprising thing.

Check your answers on page 148 and make corrections if necessary, then do the exercises on the following page.

◀◀   **Replay 7D. Listen to the conversation again.**

- Where does Ann pause when listing the items she bought at the sports store?
- Where do both speakers pause when saying the phone number?

Revision – Using intonation to show surprise

◀◀   **Replay 7D. Listen to the conversation again.**

Mark where Bob underline{repeats} information with rising intonation to show surprise.

Check your answers on page 148, then practise the conversation with a partner.

Distinguishing between the sounds /ɜ:/ and /ɔ:/ in fluent speech

Find and underline the words which are different in sentences a) and b) below. The first one has been done as an example.

👂 **7E   Listen and tick ✔ the sentence, a) or b), that you hear.**

1) ☐ a) I worked for a long time today.
   ☐ b) I walked for a long time today.

2) ☐ a) He was first to say he was wrong.
   ☐ b) He was forced to say he was wrong.

3) ☐ a) You bought a new bird yesterday.
   ☐ b) You bought a new board yesterday.

4) ☐ a) How much are the blue shirts?
   ☐ b) How much are the blue shorts?

5) ☐ a) I need to check a word in the dictionary.
   ☐ b) I need to check a 'award' in the dictionary.

6) ☐ a) I'm going to work in the park tomorrow.
   ☐ b) I'm going to walk in the park tomorrow.

7) ☐ a) I asked a lot of questions about the firm. (firm = business)
   ☐ b) I asked a lot of questions about the form. (form = written information)

Check your answers on page 148 before continuing.

Unit 11 – The World of Sport

7F Revision Exercises

⏪ **Replay 7E and listen to the sentences again. (Answers p. 149)**

Underline the stressed words in each utterance.
Draw a box around the word/s the speaker makes *most* prominent?
In which utterance does the speaker use rising intonation to show surprise.

Practise pronouncing the sentences in 7E correctly. Work with a partner.

- One person should say sentence a) or b).

- The other person should decide which sentence he/she hears.

Review – Long Vowel Sounds

Long vowel sounds - /ɑ:/, /ɜ:/ and /ɔ:/

1A Listen to the underlined vowel sounds in the following words.

Write the words in the correct columns below according to the underlined sound.

form	firm	farm	occurred	a card	accord
star	stir	store	hurt	heart	
burn	barn	born			

/ɑ:/ as in *far*	/ɜ:/ as in *fur*	/ɔ:/ as in *four*

Underline the words which are different in the sentences a), b) and c) below.

1B Listen and tick ✔ the sentence that you hear.

1)
    a) ☐ What did you think of the farm?
    b) ☐ What did you think of the firm?
    c) ☐ What did you think of the form?

2)
    a) ☐ Did you see the bar?
    b) ☐ Did you see the burr?
    c) ☐ Did you see the bore?

3)
    a) ☐ He was fast to do it.
    b) ☐ He was first to do it.
    c) ☐ He was forced to do it.

4)
    a) ☐ It's a card.
    b) ☐ It's occurred.
    c) ☐ It's a cord.

Unit 12
Options and Goals

Do you have goals?

What are your options?

What is needed to achieve your goals?

In this unit you will:

- Discuss the topic of Options and Goals.

- Practise distinguishing between the vowel sounds in the words *cot* and *coat* and to revise the sound /ɔ:/ as in the word *caught*

- Analyse the link between spoken and written English

- Examine the use of pausing in spoken language to indicate 'thought groups'

Preliminary Listening

👂 **Listen to the vowel sounds in the following words. Can you hear the difference?**

1) cot	rod	wok
2) court	roared	walk
3) coat	road	woke

Note: The third sound in each group is a diphthong sound, usually represented as /əʊ/ or /oʊ/.

As sounds are represented with various symbols in dictionaries, check the words in your dictionary now. What symbols does your dictionary use?

Part 1 - Introduction to the topic

Think about the topic before turning the page to read and listen to the text.

The speaker will talk about *Options and Goals*. What do you think the speaker will say?

☐ a) People need a plan in order to achieve their goal.

or

☐ b) People usually need some money to achieve their goal.

Check your answer by listening to Part 1A.

In Part 1, focus on *what* the speaker says about the topic.
You will focus on *how* words are pronounced in Part 2.

1A   Listen as you read the text about *Option and Goals*.

Options and Goals

What's the difference between an <u>option</u> and a <u>goal</u>? An option is a choice between more than one possible way or decision. A goal, on the other hand, is the object of a person's future plan. It's what a person wants and hopes for in the future. Most people hope for good things in the future but not everyone has a goal. Reaching a goal involves more than just talking about what we want. It involves a plan of action. It also involves focussing on the goal and having <u>strong</u> <u>motivation</u>.

A lot of people are not sure about their goals. They may know they want to do a university <u>course</u>, get a better job, go overseas or one day own a home of their own, but they don't really have a plan; they just hope that one day it'll happen. But hopes don't always <u>evolve</u>, unless we plan for them and then <u>focus</u> on the goal.

Confidence in your own ability to reach your goal is also important, as the following <u>quote</u> by Henry Ford shows:

   '*If you think you can, or if you think you can't, you're probably right.*'

1B   Write the underlined words in the text next to the correct meaning below.

1) a choice   _____   5) the target, aim   _____

2) not weak   _____   6) clearly see/give attention to   _____

3) a series of lessons _____   7) great interest in doing (something) _____

4) develop   _____   8) information repeated or copied
                                                  from another person   _____

1B   Listen and check your answers to 1B. Repeat the words after the speaker.

1C   Discuss the following questions.

   1) What's an option?

   2) What's a goal?

   3) What's needed to achieve a goal?

Unit 12 – Options and Goals

Part 2 - Focus on Pronunciation

🎧 2A Listen to the underlined vowel sound in the following words.

This unit reviews the sound /ɔː/ (sp<u>or</u>t) and examines two additional sounds, /ɒ/ (sp<u>o</u>t) and /əʊ/ (s<u>o</u>).

<u>o</u>ption	m<u>ore</u>	g<u>oa</u>l	j<u>o</u>b	c<u>our</u>se	f<u>o</u>cus
str<u>o</u>ng	<u>a</u>lways	kn<u>ow</u>	ev<u>o</u>lve	t<u>a</u>lk	qu<u>o</u>te	sh<u>ow</u>s

✎ **Write the words in the correct lists below, according to the underlined sound.**
Don't be confused by spelling. You need to listen to the *pronunciation* of the words!

1) vowel sound in the word *cot*	2) vowel sound in the word *court*	3) diphthong sound as in *coat*
option	*more*	*goal*

Check your answers on page 150.

Pausing between 'thought groups'

In this unit you will examine the way speakers *make long pieces of spoken language easier* for their listeners to understand by pausing to show where one idea or 'thought' finishes and another idea or thought starts.

A group of words that the speaker believes 'go together' as one piece of information is referred to as a 'thought group' (or 'tone unit'). Sometimes one sentence contains one thought group, but sometimes a sentence contains several thought groups.

Speakers give signals to their listeners about which pieces of information 'go together' by pausing between the thought groups.

🎧 2B Listen to the following quote from the *Options and Goals* text.

Notice how the speaker divides the sentence into three *'thought groups'* by pausing.
Draw a line / where you hear the speaker pause.

'If you think you can, or if you think you can't, you're probably right.'

Check your answer on page 150. Did you hear the pause in the correct place? If not, listen again.

The speaker's intention and the context of the situation will influence how the speaker pauses, and which words are made prominent in each thought group.

- Public speakers tend to speak more slowly and pause more frequently than speakers in informal conversation.

- Where a speaker chooses to pause will depend on which information he or she believes goes together and which parts of the message are most important.

Part 3 - Extending the topic

3A Listen to the extended text on *Options and Goals*.

Notice where the speaker pauses. He will pause where you see a comma or full stop but he will also pause to give prominence to information that he wants his listeners to notice.

Options and Goals

What's the difference between an option and a goal? An option is a choice between more than one possible way or decision. A goal, on the other hand, is the object of a person's future plan. It's what a person wants and hopes for in the future. Most people hope for good things in the future but not everyone has a goal. Reaching a goal involves more than just talking about what we want. It involves a plan of action. It also involves focussing on the goal and having strong motivation.

A lot of people are not sure about their goals. They may know they want to do a university course, get a better job, go overseas or one day own a home of their own, but they don't really have a plan; they just hope that one day it'll happen. But hopes don't always evolve, unless we plan for them and then focus on the goal.

Confidence in your own ability to reach your goal is also important, as the following quote by Henry Ford shows:

'If you think you can, or if you think you can't, you're probably right.'

The process of reaching your goal involves several important steps:

1) Decide *what* you want or hope for, by writing a list of the pros and cons of all your options. When you've reached a decision, write down your goal.

2) Decide *when* you want to achieve your goal. Be practical about this.
   Ask yourself: What's possible? What's not possible?

3) Give thought to the steps you'll need to take to reach your goal.
   What knowledge are you going to need to achieve your goal?
   What obstacles and problems will you need to overcome?
   Generally problems won't stop you reaching your goal, if you stay focussed.
   In fact, overcoming problems can often make your resolve stronger.

4) Divide your long term goal into several short term goals.
   Then focus on your short term goals.

5) Be positive about your progress. Don't only look at how far you need to go;
   also look at how far you've already progressed along the road toward your goal!

3B Extending your vocabulary

Find and <u>underline</u> the following words in the text, after the quote by Henry Ford.

pr<u>o</u>cess	pr<u>o</u>s and c<u>o</u>ns	p<u>o</u>ssible	kn<u>o</u>wledge	<u>o</u>bstacles
w<u>o</u>n't	res<u>o</u>lve	l<u>o</u>ng (term)	p<u>o</u>sitive	r<u>oa</u>d

Write the words you have underlined in the text next to the correct meaning below.
One has been done as an example.

1) advantages and disadvantages
   of an action or decision   *pros and cons*

2) confident, definite   _____

3) the path/way of going   _____

4) method of doing something   _____

5) may be achieved   _____

6) information gained by
   learning   _____

7) will not   _____

8) problems   _____

9) a strong mental decision _____

10) relating to a long
    period of time   _____

3B   **Listen and check your answers to 3B. Repeat the words after the speaker.**

Part 4 - Analysing the sounds

Replay 3B and listen to the pronunciation of the stressed syllable in each word.
Write the words in the correct columns below, then check your answers on page 151.

Note that both sounds are represented in the expression 'pr<u>o</u>s and c<u>o</u>ns'.

1) Words with the vowel sound as in *c<u>o</u>t*	2) Words with the vowel sound as in *c<u>oa</u>t*
(pros and) c<u>o</u>ns	*pr<u>o</u>s (and cons)*

Part 5 - Understanding the link between spoken and written English

Spelling Lists - Ways of *spelling the vowel sound* in the word *c<u>o</u>t*

o	a	ow
str<u>o</u>ng	w<u>a</u>nt	kn<u>ow</u>ledge
<u>o</u>bject (noun)	wh<u>a</u>t	ackn<u>ow</u>ledge
l<u>o</u>ng	w<u>as</u>	

Spelling Lists - Ways of *spelling the sound* in the word *c<u>oa</u>t*

o	oa	ow	o...e
f<u>o</u>cus	g<u>oa</u>l	foll<u>ow</u>	h<u>o</u>pe
<u>o</u>nly	r<u>oa</u>d	kn<u>ow</u>	ph<u>o</u>ne
w<u>o</u>n't	coast	sh<u>ow</u>	qu<u>o</u>te

Note: For ways of spelling the sound /ɔː/ as in *sp<u>or</u>t* and *c<u>a</u>ll*, see Unit 11, Part 5.

Part 6 - Spelling Check – Dictation

Listen to the text about *Options and Goals* again.

Complete the text with the correct words. (Pause the recording to write the words.)

Options and Goals

What's the difference between an _____ and a goal? An option is a choice between more than one possible way or decision. A goal, on the other hand, is the _____ of a person's future plan. It's what a person wants and _____ for in the future. _____ people hope for good things in the future but not everyone has a goal. Reaching a goal involves _____ than just talking about what we _____. It involves a plan of action. It also involves focussing on the goal and having _____ motivation.

A _____ of people are not sure about their goals. They may _____ they want to do a university _____, get a better job, go overseas or one day _____ a home of their own, but they _____ really have a plan; they just hope that one day it'll happen. But hopes don't always evolve, unless we plan for them and then _____ on the goal.

Part 7 - Listening Practice – 'thought groups'

7A Listen to the conversation between friends.

Notice where the speakers pause to signal 'thought groups'?
Draw a line / where the speakers pause. The first line has been done as an example.

Note: Informal speech is generally spoken more quickly than carefully read text so there will be fewer pauses.

Joan: /You know how I've been talking about going overseas?

Bob: You're always talking about it.

Joan: Well, I've decided to make a goal to go in November.

Bob: November? It's already August. That's only four months off. How will you afford it?

Joan: Well I've set myself some goals. I'm going to quit smoking, make a lot less phone calls, walk more instead of using public transport. And I'm going to do more overtime at work. By October I should have enough money to go.

Bob: Quit smoking? Walk more? Are you joking? I've heard all this before.

Joan: I know but this time I feel very motivated. So…If I can stay focussed on the goal I know I'll be in Rome by the end of November. Mm … I'll have to start thinking about clothes. Is it hot or cold in Rome in November?

Bob: Mm I'm not sure. It'll be cold I think.

Revision exercises

◄◄ Replay 7A   Mark where linking occurs between words ‿ in each utterance.

Remember – linking doesn't generally occur where speakers pause.

(If necessary, review the information about word linking in Unit 7.)

◄◄ **Replay 7A - Mark where Bob <u>repeats</u> information with rising intonation to show surprise.**

Check your answers for 7A, then practise the conversation with a partner.

7B Listen to the English pronunciation of the following place names.

eg. W<u>a</u>shington *city*	S<u>eou</u>l _____	Sc<u>o</u>tland _____
R<u>o</u>me _____	P<u>o</u>land _____	Osl<u>o</u> _____	Cair<u>o</u> _____
Quit<u>o</u> _____	Mong<u>o</u>lia _____	Toky<u>o</u> _____	Cong<u>o</u> _____

Use an atlas to locate the places. Which places are cities? Which places are countries? Write *country* or *city* next to each place, as in the example above.

◄◄ **Replay 7B and listen to the place names again.**

7C Write the place names in the columns below, according to the <u>underlined</u> sound.

1) Places with the vowel sound as in *c<u>o</u>t*	2) Places with the vowel sound as in *c<u>oa</u>t*

Is it warm or cold at the end of November?

Joan is hoping to go to each of the above places between the end of November and March. She wants to know which places are generally warm and which are generally cold at that time of the year? (ie. Cold enough to need warm clothes in the early morning.) Use an atlas to help decide the answer.

7D Write your answers in the correct column below.

Hot/warm - November to March	Cold - November to March

Check your answers on page 152 before continuing.

Write sentences in your notebook using the following structure:

It's generally *cold* in *Tokyo* between November and March.

Read your sentences aloud to practise the pronunciation.

Distinguishing between sounds in fluent speech

<u>Underline</u> the words which are different in sentences a) and b) below.
The first one has been done as an example.

7E **Listen and tick** ✔ **the sentence, a) or b) that you hear.**

1) ☐ a) I'd like to buy a <u>cot</u>, please.
   ☐ b) I'd like to buy a <u>coat</u>, please.

2) ☐ a) I can't find the right rod.
   ☐ b) I can't find the right road.

3) ☐ a) He told me about the cost.
   ☐ b) He told me about the coast.

4) ☐ a) She hops every day to get slimmer.
   ☐ b) She hopes every day to get slimmer.

5) ☐ a) How do you spell 'rob'?
   ☐ b) How do you spell 'robe'?

6) ☐ a) Can you help me with this knot?
   ☐ b) Can you help me with this note?

7) ☐ a) The students want Elle. (Note: Elle is a girl's name)
   ☐ b) The students won't tell.

7) ☐ a) They want work.
   ☐ b) They won't work.

◀◀ **Replay 7E on the audio recording and listen again.**
Pause the recording after each utterance to do the following exercises

7F <u>Underline</u> **the words with stressed syllables.**
Draw a box **around the word/s the speakers make** *most prominent* **in each sentence.**

Check your answers on page 152 before continuing.

Practise pronouncing the sentences correctly. Work with a partner.

• One person should say sentence a) or b).

• The other person should decide which sentence he/she hears.

Part 8 - Practising what you have learnt

Write a few sentences about *your* goals or interview another student about their goals and then write a short report. Try to include some of the following words:

hope to	goal	going to	short-term	long-term	want to

Use sentence patterns such as:

My short-term goal is to (+ verb)...........   or   (Rona's) goal is to (+ verb).......
I am going to (+ verb)...........   (Rona) is going to (+ verb)........
I hope to (+verb) ....   (Rona) hopes to (+ verb)..........

Now look at the sentences you have written.
When changing the information from *written sentences* to *spoken language:*

* Which word or words would you make prominent in each sentence or thought group?

* Where would you use contractions?

* Which words would be weak or unstressed?

* Where would you pause?

* Where would you link words?

Practise saying the information in a natural way. If possible, record yourself so you can listen to your pronunciation. Ask a fluent speaker of English to comment on your pronunciation.

My long-term goal's to travel all over the world. In order to do that, I'm going to do a course on teaching English so I can work as I go. So my short term goals are to get a qualification and...

Concluding Progress Check

Listening Test - Exercise 1

🕉 **Listen and tick ☑ the sentence (a) or (b) that you hear.**

(The first one has been done as an example.)

1)
☐ a) They're <u>living</u> on a boat.
☑ b) They're <u>leaving</u> on a boat.

2)
☐ a) I left my <u>cap</u> in the kitchen.
☐ b) I left my <u>cup</u> in the kitchen.

3)
☐ a) Have they <u>packed</u> the car yet?
☐ b) Have they <u>parked</u> the car yet?

4)
☐ a) How do you spell '<u>full</u>'?
☐ b) How do you spell '<u>fool</u>'?

5)
☐ a) I need a <u>desk</u> for my computer.
☐ b) I need a <u>disk</u> for my computer.

6)
☐ a) Did you see the little boy's <u>mouth</u>?
☐ b) Did you see the little boy's <u>mouse</u>?

7)
☐ a) How many <u>pairs</u> did you see?
☐ b) How many <u>bears</u> did you see?

8)
☐ a) Where's the <u>pen</u>?
☐ b) Where's the <u>pain</u>?

9)
☐ a) I <u>worked</u> for a long time today.
☐ b) I <u>walked</u> for a long time today.

10)
☐ a) Did he finish his <u>rice</u>?
☐ b) Did he finish his <u>race</u>?

11)
☐ a) They <u>want</u> work.
☐ b) They <u>won't</u> work.

12)
☐ a) They went the <u>long</u> way.
☐ b) They went the <u>wrong</u> way.

13)
☐ a) The <u>men</u> listened to the story.
☐ b) The <u>man</u> listened to the story.

Listening Test - Exercise 2

In English, word stress helps the listener to recognise words correctly.
The following words are spelt the same but are stressed differently, producing different meanings.

🕉 **Listen and tick ☑ the word (a) or (b) that you hear.** (The stressed part is <u>underlined</u>.)

1)
☐ a) <u>pre</u>sent
☐ b) pre<u>sent</u>

2)
☐ a) <u>ob</u>ject
☐ b) ob<u>ject</u>

3)
☐ a) <u>de</u>sert
☐ b) de<u>sert</u>

4)
☐ a) <u>pro</u>duce
☐ b) pro<u>duce</u>

Listening Test - Exercise 3

🦻 **Listen and <u>underline</u> the words that are stressed by the speakers.**

The first sentence has been done as an example.
If necessary, pause the recording after each line.

A: Could you <u>tell</u> me where the <u>bank</u> is <u>please</u>?

B: Yes, in High Street, on the left, near the library.

A: Thanks. And is there somewhere to park the car?

B: Yes. There's a place just next to the bank but you'll have to pay.

A: Oh. Do you know what they charge?

B: I don't, I'm sorry - but there'll be a sign at the gate with the price.

       There's also a place near the station. It's usually full but you could check.

A: OK. Thanks for your help.

Listening Test – Exercise 4

🦻 **Listen and write what the speakers say.**

(Pause the recording after each line while you write the sentence.)

1) _____

2) _____

3) _____

4) _____

5) _____

Part 3

Listening Test - Exercise 1

1) b) They're <u>leaving</u> on a boat.
2) b) I left my <u>cup</u> in the kitchen.
3) a) Have they <u>packed</u> the car yet?
4) a) How do you spell '<u>full</u>?
5) b) I need a <u>disk</u> for my computer.
6) a) Did you see the little boy's <u>mouth</u>?

7) b) How many <u>bears</u> did you see?
8) b) Where's the <u>pain</u>?
9) a) I <u>worked</u> for a long time today.
10) a) Did he finish his <u>rice</u>?
11) a) They <u>want</u> work.
12) b) They went the <u>wrong</u> way.
13) a) The <u>men</u> listened to the story.

Listening Test - Exercise 2

1) a) <u>present</u>
2) b) ob<u>ject</u>

3) a) <u>desert</u>
4) b) pro<u>duce</u>

Listening Test - Exercise 3

A: Could you <u>tell</u> me where the <u>bank is please</u>?

B: <u>Yes</u>, in <u>High</u> Street, on the <u>left</u>, near the <u>library</u>.

A: <u>Thanks</u>. And is there <u>some</u>where to <u>park</u> the <u>car</u>?

B: There's a <u>place</u> just <u>next</u> to the <u>bank</u> but you'll have to <u>pay</u>.

A: Oh. Do you <u>know</u> what they <u>charge</u>?

B: I <u>don't,</u> I'm <u>sorry</u> - but there'll be a <u>sign</u> at the <u>gate</u> with the <u>price</u>.

       There's also a <u>place</u> near the <u>station</u>. It's usually <u>full</u> but you could <u>check</u>.

A: OK. <u>Thanks</u> for your <u>help</u>.

Listening Test – Exercise 4

In sentences with contractions, both the contracted form and the full form have been given below. Either answer can be counted as correct – however, notice that the speakers on the audio recording use contractions. For information about contractions, see Unit 2, Part 8A.

1) What's your phone number?
   (What is your phone number?)   (five words)

2) How do you spell your surname?   (six words)

3) I'll check on the computer.
   (I will check on the computer.)   (six words)

4) I can send some information if you're interested.
   (I can send some information if you are interested.)   (nine words)

5) I'd like to speak to someone now if possible.
   (I would like to speak to someone now if possible.)   (ten words)

Part 1- Introduction to the topic
b) When studying a new language it's important to remember that making mistakes is a natural part of learning.

1B

1) difficult & new experience	*challenge*	6)	level/grade	*standard*
2) way of pronunciation	*accent*	7)	subject/situation	*matter*
3) speak <u>unc</u>learly, quietly	*mutter*	8)	not active	*passive*
4) be the same as	*match*	9)	problems	*trouble*
5) easy/ with no trouble	*comfortable*	10)	unknown/new	*unfamiliar*

1C

3) Some language learners worry very much if listeners have trouble understanding their accent or when people mutter expressions they don't understand.
4) A plan of action and regular practice
5) Being an active, rather than a passive learner means using every opportunity to practise your language skills and being prepared to ask for help and correction.

Part 2A

1) Sound /æ/ as in the word *fan*		2) Sound /ʌ / as in the word *fun*	
challenge	*plan*	*some*	*mutter*
accent	*practise*	*worry*	*other*
standard	*match*	*much*	*cultures*
matter	*active*	*trouble*	

2C

some	1	*worry*	2	*challenge*	2
much	1	*trouble*	2	*accent*	2
mutter	2	*standard*	2	*matter*	2
plan	1	*practise*	2	*match*	1
active	2	*other*	2	*cultures*	2

Part 3B

1) have the use of (something)	*access (to)*	6) fortune	*luck*
2) person who examines in detail	*analyst*	7) group, set	*category*
3) main organ of speech	*tongue*	8) way of thinking	*attitude*
4) become used to new condition	*adapt*	9) assist, help	*encourage*
5) absence, be without	*lack*	10) the end product	*results*
		11) quickly	*(in a) hurry*

Part 4

1) Words with the sound /æ/ (as in *fan*)		2) Words with the sound /ʌ/ (as in *fun*)	
access		*tongue*	*hurry*
analyst	*category*	*luck*	
adapt	*attitude*	*encourage*	
lack		*results*	

Part 6 Check answers against the text in Part 1A

Part 7A

1) Do you worry <u>when people don't unlerstand your accent</u>?
2) When's the best time to <u>practise a new language</u>?
3) Do you use your <u>dictionary to check pronunciation</u>?
4) How can you be <u>successful in language study</u>?

7B

1) a) The <u>fan</u> was shared by everyone.
2) b) How's your <u>uncle</u>?
3) a) Did you see the <u>track</u> near the side of the road?
4) a) They don't <u>matter</u> much, so don't worry.
5) a) She likes clothes to <u>match</u>.
6) b) The sick old man <u>muttered</u> to the kind doctor.
7) b) Where could I buy a new <u>cup</u>?
8) b) They found a <u>hut</u> in the forest.

Part 8A

Contractions	Number of syllables		Negative Contractions	Number of syllables
I'm	1		isn't	2
He's	1		aren't	1
She's	1		weren't	1
It's	1		can't	1
There's	1		couldn't	2
			don't	1
			won't	1
You're	1			
We're /weə/	1	(or can be 2 syllables when pronounced /wiːə/)		
They're /ðeə/	1	(or can be 2 syllables when pronounced /ðeɪə/)		
I'd	1			
He'd	1			
They'd	1			
It'd	2			
I'll	1			
You'll	1			
It'll	2			
I've	1			
You've	1			
We've	1			
They've	1			

8B

a) Contractions are used <u>nine</u> times in Part 3A.
b) *don't, it's, you'll,* are pronounced as one syllable;
   isn't is pronounced as two syllables.

Part 1 Introduction to the topic
b) Many people think that learning about other cultures can be educational and rewarding.

1B 1) standards/ideas about what
    is important   *values*
   2) useful for learning   *educational*
   3) willing to accept new ideas *open-minded*

4) satisfying, worthwhile *rewarding*
5) know well   *familiar with*
6) life times   *generations*

1C
   1) Culture means the way of living of a particular group of people
   2) People from different cultures grow up with different customs, beliefs and values.
      Culture is usually passed from parents to children for many generations.

Part 2B

eg. /ə/ *people*   /ə/ *problem*   /ə/ *collect*   /ə/ *listen*   /ə/ *pattern*   /ə/ *along*   /ə/ *second*

2D - Listening Exercise 5

1) The speaker is stressing every word. The listener can't hear which words are important
    to the message.
2) The speaker can make his message clearer by stressing only the important information words.

2D - Listening Exercise 6
I'd <u>like</u> you to <u>meet</u> the <u>man</u>ager of the de<u>part</u>ment for <u>cul</u>tural edu<u>ca</u>tion.
             ('*I would*' is usually contracted to *I'd* in spoken language).

Part 3B
1) stay away from   *avoid*
2) good/OK/appropriate   *acceptable*
3) bad, insulting   *offensive*
4) open-minded, willing to
   listen to other opinions *tolerant*

5) happen   *occur*
6) know about/understand *aware (of)*
7) stopped before it happens *prevented*

8) way of doing, acting *behaviour*

Part 4
eg. /ə/ ac/<u>cep</u>/ta/ble   /ə/ /ə/ a/<u>void</u> (2 syllables)   /ə/ o/<u>ffen</u>/sive (3 syllables)   /ə/ /ə/ <u>to</u>/le/rant (3 syllables)

/ə/ o/<u>ccur</u> (2 syllables)   /ə/ a/<u>ware</u> (2 syllables)   /ə/ /ə/ pre/<u>vent</u>/ed (3 syllables)   /ə/ /ə/ be<u>hav</u>iour (3 syllables)

Part 7A
     1) Where are you from?
     2) Do you like it here?   3) How is it different from your country?

7B
1) <u>Where</u> /ə/ are you /ə/ <u>from</u>?   The words with stressed syllables (important information) are <u>underlined</u>.
                       The *un*stressed words are shown with /ə/.
2) /ə/ /ə/ <u>Do</u> you <u>like</u> /ə/ it <u>here</u>?
3) /ə/ <u>How's</u> it /ə/ /ə/ <u>diff</u>erent /ə/ from <u>your</u> <u>country</u>? (Note: 'different' can also be pronounced with 2 syllables: /dɪfrənt/

9B
Do you <u>think</u> /θ/ everyone in <u>the</u> /ð/ world should do <u>things</u> /θ/ as you do <u>them</u> /ð/ in your culture or

are you open-minded about o<u>ther</u> /ð/ customs? Most people believe <u>that</u> /ð/ learning about

o<u>ther</u> /ð/ cultures can be educational and rewarding.

9D
    1) a) He said <u>something</u> better than them.
    2) a) Did you see the little boy's <u>mouth</u>?

3) b) He <u>taught</u> for a long time.
4) a) I'd like to order two <u>thin</u> boxes, please.

Part 1 - Introduction to the topic
a) Many country people think city living is <u>artificial</u> compared to country living.

Part 1B

1) nervous/uneasy	<u>*ill at ease*</u>	6) often	<u>*frequently*</u>
2) good chances	<u>*opportunities*</u>	7) not natural	<u>*artificial*</u>
3) age between 13 to 19 years	<u>*teens*</u>	8) dangerous	<u>*risky*</u>
4) showed	<u>*revealed*</u>	9) healthy/strong	<u>*fit*</u>
5) judged before knowing facts	<u>*preconceived*</u>	10) building for indoor sport and exercise	<u>*gym*</u>

Part 1C - Answers are in the text. Possible answers are:

1) People live near cities because there are more opportunities for business and study.
2) Some country people believe that city living is artificial, and risky and that city people aren't as fit as country people.

Part 2A

1 Sound /ɪ/ as in the word ship	2 Sound /iː/ as in the word sheep
th<u>i</u>s *artif<u>i</u>cial* *b<u>u</u>siness* *g<u>y</u>m* *l<u>i</u>ving* *f<u>i</u>t* *f<u>i</u>ll* *r<u>i</u>sky* *<u>i</u>s* (When unstressed, 'is' is pronounced /əz/)	*t<u>ee</u>ns* *<u>ea</u>se* *l<u>ea</u>ving* *preconc<u>ei</u>ved* *f<u>ee</u>l* *th<u>e</u>se* *rev<u>ea</u>led* *frequ<u>e</u>ntly* *bel<u>ie</u>ve*

Part 2B Syllables and word stress

words with one syllable	words with two syllables	words with three syllables	words with four syllables
th<u>i</u>s *gym* *teens* *these* *fill* *fit* *feel* *is* *ease*	<u>*business*</u> *('i' is not pronounced in business)* <u>*living*</u> <u>*leaving*</u> *re<u>vealed</u>* *be<u>lieve</u>* <u>*risky*</u>	*preconceived** <u>*frequently*</u> **primary stress is on the final syllable, secondary stress is on the first syllable*	*artif<u>i</u>cial*

Part 3B

1) pictures or ideas	<u>*images*</u>	6) feel comfortable	<u>*at ease*</u>
2) people guilty of crime	<u>*criminals*</u>	7) say hello	<u>*greet*</u>
3) show, describe	<u>*depict*</u>	8) people who steal	<u>*thieves*</u>
4) television, radio, newspapers	<u>*media*</u>	9) easy, handy	<u>*convenient*</u>
5) causing false belief	<u>*deceiving*</u>	10) totally, 100%	<u>*completely*</u>

Part 4

1) Words with the sound /ɪ/ (as in ship)	2) Words with the sound /iː/ (as in sheep)		
<u>i</u>mages *cr<u>i</u>minal* *dep<u>i</u>ct*	*th<u>ie</u>ves* *m<u>e</u>dia* *dec<u>ei</u>ving*	*<u>ea</u>se* *gr<u>ee</u>t* *conv<u>e</u>nient*	*compl<u>e</u>tely*

Part 7A

1) *Do you live in a city?*
2) *What do you like* most *about living in the city?*
3) *What do you like* least *about living in the city?*

7B 1) Do you <u>live</u> in a <u>city</u>? (Note: Auxiliary verbs such as *do, have, has,* are often *un*stressed.)

2) <u>What</u> do you <u>like</u> <u>most</u> about <u>living</u> in the <u>city</u>?

3) <u>What</u> do you <u>like</u> <u>least</u> about <u>living</u> in the <u>city</u>?

7C 1) Do you <u>live</u> in a [city]?   Note: Stressed words are <u>underlined</u>.

2) <u>What</u> do you <u>like</u> [most] about <u>living</u> in the <u>city</u>?   Prominent words are in a [box]

3) <u>What</u> do you <u>like</u> [least] about <u>living</u> in the <u>city</u>?

7E 1) b) Do they sell beans ?   6) a) I've never seen this before.

2) a) They're living on a boat.   7) b) It's easy to sleep in here.

3) a) Can you see the ship near the rocks?   8) b) Did you feel it?

4) b) That was a very good peach!   9) b) How easy!

5) a) You must hit the metal to make it bend.

7F 1) b) Do they <u>sell</u> [beans] ?   6) a) I've <u>never</u> seen [this] <u>before</u>.

2) a) They're <u>living</u> on a [boat].   7) b) It's [easy] to <u>sleep</u> in <u>here</u>.

3) a) Can you <u>see</u> the [ship] <u>near</u> the [rocks]?   8) b) [Did] you [feel] it?

4) b) [That] was a [very] good [peach]!   9) b) [How] [easy]!

5) a) You must [hit] the <u>metal</u> to <u>make</u> it <u>bend</u>.   Note: Stressed words are <u>underlined</u>.
          Prominent words are in a [box]

Parts 8A and 8B

Manilla /ɪ/ *city- capital of the Philippines* Syria /ɪ/ *country* Greece /iː/ *country* Lima /iː/ *city, capital of Peru*

England /ɪ/ *country* Madrid /ɪ/ *city* Egypt /iː/ *country* Quito /iː/ *city*

Sweden /iː/ *country* Lisbon /ɪ/ *city, capital of Portugal* Sydney /ɪ/ *city- capital of NSW, Australia*

8C and 8D

A: If <u>you</u> could <u>live</u> in [any] city you <u>wished</u>, <u>which</u> city would you [pick]?

B: <u>That's</u> [easy]. [Madrid].

A: [Madrid].

B: <u>Yes,</u> [definitely]. I <u>think</u> <u>Madrid</u>'s a [fascinating] place.
And <u>which</u> <u>city</u> would [you] [pick]?   Note: Stressed words are <u>underlined</u>.

A: It'd <u>have</u> to be [Sydney].   Prominent words are in a [box]

B: [Really].

A: <u>Yes</u> – it's <u>always</u> been my [dream] to <u>live</u> in <u>Sydney</u>.   Note: The pronunciation of 'been' in this
          sentence is weak: /bɪn/

Part 9A

1) When's the train to the [city] due?

2) [When]'s the train to the city due?

3) When's the [train] to the city due?

4) When's the train [to] the city due?

9B

a) The speaker wants to know about *when* the train will arrive, not *where* it will arrive.   **2**

b) The speaker wants to know about trains to the *city*, not trains to the *country*.   **1**

c) The speaker wants to know about trains *to* the city, not *from* the city.   **4**

d) The speaker wants to know about the *train*, not the *bus*.   **3**

Part 1- Introduction to the topic

b) National Parks have been established to protect the world's natural marvels.

1B

1) having few (people)	*sparsely*		6) sensible, wise	*far-sighted*
2) quick	*rapid*		7) homes/places of living	*habitats*
3) badly marked	*scarred*		8) organised action	*campaigns*
4) bad management	*mismanagement*		9) disappear/die	*vanish*
5) increased, become bigger	*expanded*		10) wonderful things	*marvels*

1C 1) The land has been clear for farming housing and mining. Large areas of land have been scarred and damged.

2) Yellowstone, in the United States of America.

Part 2A

1 Sound /æ/ as in the word *pack*	2 Sound /ɑ:/ as in the word *park*
expanded *natural* *rapid* *began* *vanish* *habitats*	*sparsely* *marvels* *scarred* *started* *far-sighted*

2B

ed pronounced as /əd/	*ed* pronounced as /t/	*ed* pronounced as /d/
expanded *started* *populated* *far-sighted* *needed*	*established* *walked* *packed*	*caused* *damaged* *scarred* *happened*

Part 3B

1) plan of management	*strategy*		6) die of hunger	*starve*
2) dried/burnt	*parched*		7) easily damaged	*fragile*
3) balance, agreement	*harmony*		8) not producing	*barren*
4) useful, valuable things	*assets*		9) not allowing	*banning*
5) places of protection	*sanctuaries*		10) protecting	*guarding*

Part 4

1) Words with the sound /æ/ (as in pack)	2) Words with the sound /ɑ:/ (as in park)
strategy *assets* *barren* *sanctuaries* *banning* *fragile*	*parched* *harmony* *starve* *guarding*

Part 6 Check answers against the text in Part 1A

Part 7

Q1) What do you think about national parks? *Do you think they're* necessary?

Q2) *Have you ever visited* one?

Q3) Galapagos? *Is that in* South America?

Q4) Oh, I see…*What did you do when you were there*?

Q5) Yes, I can imagine…What other places *would you like to visit*?

7A – Prominent words are shown within a box.
The stressed syllable in prominent words with more than one syllable is shaded.

1) Q: What do you think about national parks? Do you think they're necessary?
   A: Absolutely - without them many animals'd vanish.
2) Q: Have you ever visited one?
   A: Yes, I've been to Galapagos and that was spectacular.
3) Q: Galapagos? Is that in South America?
   A: No, it's a group of islands off the west coast. It's part of Ecuador.
4) Q: Oh, I see…What did you do when you were there?
   A: Well, there're no large land animals on Galapagos but we did get to see an albatross and that was fantastic.
5) Q: Yes, I can imagine….What other places would you like to visit?
   A: I'd love to travel to Africa and go on safari and see antelope and black rhino
      That'd be fantastic! - and Antarctica - I think Antarctica'd be spectacular.

7B

Q) Is Bamff National Park in Africa?   A) No, its in Canada.
Q) Is Akan National Park in Canada?   A) No, it's in Japan.
Q) Is Mana Pools National Park in Japan?   A) No, it's in Africa.

7C   1 a) There was a lamb on the road.

2 b) Have they parked the car yet?

3 a) She wore a white dress, with a blue hat.

4 a) That dog needs its back checked!

5 b) Did you see the cart on the road?

6 a) The children watched the match.

7D1)   1) There was a lamb on the road.

2) Have they parked the car yet?

3) She wore a white dress with a blue hat.

4) That dog needs its back checked!

5) Did you see the cart on the road?

6) The children watched the match.

7D2) The words *parked, checked, watched,* are each pronounced as one syllable.

Part 8A
Conversation 1   *I've just come back from a trip to Kakadu.*
                 It was spectacular   *Kakadu? Is that in Africa?*

Conversation 2
                 It was difficult. I need to practise   *This afternoon?*
How was your exam, Mark? *more before the next exam.*   *Do you need some help to study?*
                 It starts this afternoon.

Part 9C   1) b) How many bears did you see?
                2) a) Have you packed the car yet?

Exercise 1

1) b) They <u>mutter</u> too much.

2) b) I'll need a <u>cab</u> today.

3) a) Did you <u>fill</u> it?

4) a) How many <u>pairs</u> did you see?

5) b) The children watched the <u>march</u>.

6) b) It's easy to <u>sleep</u> in here.

7) b) He <u>thought</u> for a long time.

Exercise 2

1) b) con<u>duct</u>

2) a) <u>a</u>vid

3) b) <u>a</u>ssert

4) b) de<u>fer</u>

Exercise 3 & 4a

1) Where did you park the car?

2) They can come with me.

3) When will the train from the city arrive?

4) The meeting will be in the city on Sunday.

Exercise 4b

4 Giving new information.

1 Asking for new information

3 Checking information already talked about?

2 Making an offer.

Unit 6 - Books and Computers - Answers

Part 1- Introduction to the topic

a) Computers are used by students in most schools and universities.

1B
1) opinion	*view*	6) simple/easy to use	*user-friendly*	
2) period of time as a child	*childhood*	7) good chances	*opportunities*	
3) answers	*solutions*	8) regularly	*routinely*	
4) filled/occupied space	*took up*	9) very important	*crucial*	
5) brought into use for the first time	*introduced*	10) (for our own) benefit	*good*	

1C

1) During the 1940's

2) When the first automatic electronic computers were introduced, one computer took up a whole room and could be used by only a few skilled technicians.

3) Some people think society is *too* dependent on computer technology for its own good.

Part 2A

/ʊ/		/uː/	
full	*took*	*school*	*few*
books	*could*	*rooms* Note: some speakers pronounce as /rʊmz/	
would	*good*	*computers*	*crucial*
look		*students*	*view*

2C

Do you have childhood memories ⌣ of school rooms full ⌣ of books ⌣ or rooms full ⌣ of computers?
In the past students would look ⌣ in books for solutions to their questions, but ⌣ in schools today,
students ⌣ often look to computers for ⌣ information. Computer technology has ⌣ opened ⌣ up ⌣ a
whole new world ⌣ of communication ⌣ and ⌣ educational ⌣ opportunities. In fact, computers ⌣ are
now *used so much ⌣ it's difficult to imagine ⌣ a world without them.

* The first syllable in words beginning with the letter 'u', as in 'used', is often pronounced as /juː/.

* In the word 'imagine', the final letter 'e' is not pronounced, so 'n' links to 'a'. eg. imagine a
⌣

Part 3B   1) helpful instruments   *tools*   6) difficult to understand   *confusing*
2) very big, great   *huge*   7) make better   *improve*
3) decrease, make less   *reduce*   8) because of (something)   *due (to)*
4) using a lot of time   *time-consuming*   9) young people   *youth*
5) questions, problems *issues*

Part 4B   /uː/   /uː/   /uː/
tool, issues, improve are pronounced /uː/
/juː/   /juː/   /juː/   /juː/ /juː/ /juː/
huge, reduce, consuming, confusing, due, youth

Part 7A Q 1) *Do you think computers're* too time-consuming?
Q 2) *Do you think computers'll* reduce or increase employment in the future?
Q 3) *Do you think computers'll* completely replace books in the future?

7B Note: *'Do you'* is pronounced as one syllable, /dʒə/, in each of the following utterances.

Q 1) *Do you think ⌣ computers're* too time-consuming?
Q 2) *Do you think ⌣ computers'll* reduce ⌣ or ⌣ increase ⌣ employment ⌣ in the future?
Q 3) *Do you think ⌣ computers'll* completely replace books ⌣ in the future?

7D   2 a) How do you spell 'full'?   4 d) They could.
6 b) How do you spell 'fool'?   5 e) They cooed.
1 c) How do you spell 'fuel'   3 f) They queued.

Part 8A What ⌣ tim(e) ⌣ is ⌣ Susan ⌣ arriving?   At ⌣ ten ⌣ o' clock ⌣ in the morning.

Part 1 Introduction to the topic a) Balanced living is necessary for health and happiness.

1B 1) parts, units   _elements_   7) mental tension   _stress_
    2) people with special knowledge   _experts_   8) the way into   _access_
    3) not active   _passive_   9) time limits   _deadlines_
    4) use time   _spend_   10) leisure time   _recreation_
    5) extended over time   _spanned_   11) too much, more
    6) harmony, having equal amounts _balance_   than necessary   _excess_

1C – *possible answers*
1)   Balance in all aspects of living.
2)   *Yang* represents the active elements of the universe; *yin* represents the passive elements.
3)   Due to business or study deadlines, many people work to excess; leaving little time at the
      end of their busy day to spend with family and friends.

Part 2A

1) Sound /e/ as in the word '*send*'	2) Sound /æ/ as in the word '*sand*'
h_ea_lthy w_ea_lth sp_e_nd inst_ea_d s_ai_d m_a_ny _e_xcess	h_a_ppy b_a_lance sp_a_nned s_a_d _a_ccess

Part 3B
1) a desire to reach a goal   *ambition*   5) share or distribute   *allocate*
2) power for activity   *energy*   6) manner, style, way   *fashion*
3) calm, happy   *relaxed*   7) good result, achievement *success*
4) enjoyment, fun   *pleasure*

Part 4

Words with the sound /e/ (as in send)	Words with the sound /æ/ (as in sand)
_e_nergy pl_ea_sure succ_e_ss	_a_mbition *(Primary stress is on the second syllable /æmbɪʃən/* rel_a_xed *- secondary stress is on the first syllable)* _a_llocate f_a_shion

Part 7C

Doctor:	Now t_o a_nswer your question about your headaches Mrs West - I think /w/
	they're th_e e_ffect of tension in your neck. Have you been feeling stressed? /j/
Mrs. West:	Yes I don't seem to get time to d_o a_nything but work. /w/
Doctor:	How much time do you spend w_o_rking at your desk?
Mrs. West:	O(h) _a_bout ten hours a day on th_e a_verage. /w/ /j/
Doctor:	Well th_e o_nly _a_nswer is to take regular breaks or your headaches won't get better. /j/ /j/
Mrs. West:	Yes _I e_xpect so. /j/
Doctor:	And _I_ want t_o e_ncourage you t_o e_xercise regularly. Do you get much exercise? /j/ /w/ /w/
Mrs. West:	No I haven't had the time or th_e e_nergy t_o e_xercise. /j/ /w/
Doctor:	Well, it's important to make th_e e_ffort t_o e_xercise. Your health is your most /j/ /w/
	valuable asset and th_e o_nly way to prevent th_e e_ffects of stress is to be more balanced. /j/ /j/
Mrs. West:	So if _I e_xercise and relax more, can _I e_xpect my headaches to g_o a_way? /j/ /j/ /w/
Doctor:	Yes and _I e_xpect th_e o_ther benefit will b_e i_ncreased energy. /j/ /j/ /j/
Mrs. West:	Well I'll d_o e_verything you suggest, doctor, if it'll make me feel better. /w/
Doctor:	Good. We'll get yo_u o_n an exercise program immediately. /w/

7D 1) b) The family was sad to have lost everything.

2) a) The men listened to the explanation.

3) b) The track was difficult and dangerous.

4) b) The workers sat out in the field.

5) a) The company had an expensive plan for the future.

6) b) How much access do we have?

7E Revision exercises

1) The family was⌣sad to have lost⌣everything.

2) The men listened to the⌣explanation.

3) The track was difficult⌣and⌣dangerous.
                                      /j/

4) The workers⌣sat⌣out⌣in the field.

5) The company had⌣an⌣expensive plan

6) How much⌣access do we have?

Part 8A
            /s /   /s/   /k/   /s/   /s/   /s/   /k/
        balance   principles   active   importance   necessary   exercise   cause

8B
                              /s/   /k//s/   /k/   /k/
A: Did you hear that Cindy's been accepted into Canning College?
                                              /s/
B: No I didn't. She must be excited.
                /s/   /s/   /s/ /s/   /k/ /k/   /k/
A: She certainly is. We're going to celebrate at the City Circle Café. Can you come?
          /k/   /k/ /s/   /s/   /k/
B: No I can't cancel my appointment at the office, but please give her my congratulations.
              /k/
A: I will, of course.

Part 1 Introduction to the topic b) People now expect to live <u>longer, healthier lives</u>.

1B

1) restricted to a few	*limited*	7) repair, fix	*mend*
2) amazing	*incredible*	8) a danger	*threat*
3) ways of doing something	*methods*	9) modern, advanced	*progressive*
4) stop from happening	*prevent*	10) however/but	*nevertheless*
5) damage to the body	*physical injuries*	11) increased	*extended*
6) things designed, created	*inventions*		

1C *Possible answers are:*

1) Illnesses which, in the past, were a serious threat to many children can now be prevented. The lives of millions of men, women and children have been extended by modern medicine.

2) Long before the twenty-first century, Chinese medical books contained information on how to mix special medicines from herbs to prevent illness and mend injuries.

Part 2A

1) Sound /e/ as in the word 'when'		2) Sound /ɪ/ as in the word 'win'
m<u>e</u>thods		l<u>i</u>mited
prev<u>e</u>nt	ext<u>e</u>nded	f<u>i</u>xed
n<u>e</u>vertheless	d<u>ea</u>th	ph<u>y</u>sical
thr<u>ea</u>t	<u>a</u>ny	<u>i</u>njuries
incr<u>e</u>dible	fri<u>e</u>nd	m<u>i</u>x
m<u>e</u>nd	h<u>ea</u>lth	w<u>o</u>men

2B

words with one syllable	words with two syllables	words with three syllables	words with four syllables
fixed friend	methods	limited	nevertheless
threat health	prevent	extended	incredible
mend	any	physical	
death	women	injuries	
mix			

Part 3B

1) find, reveal	*detect*	6) increase in area	*spread*
2) people who are hurt	*victims*	7) easily infecting others	*infectious*
3) arms, legs	*limbs*	8) having the right result	*effective*
4) ability to move	*mobility*	9) signs of illness	*symptoms*
5) regular beat, pulse	*rhythm*	10) electronic objects fixed into the body	*implants*

Part 4

Words with the sound /e/ (as in *when*)	Words with the sound /ɪ/ (as in *win*)	
det<u>e</u>ct	*v<u>i</u>ctims*	*s<u>y</u>mptoms*
spr<u>ea</u>d	*l<u>i</u>mbs*	*<u>i</u>mplants*
inf<u>e</u>ctious	*mob<u>i</u>lity*	
eff<u>e</u>ctive	*rh<u>y</u>thm*	

Part 7A

A: What do you think is the most incredible medical invention?

B: You mean this century?

A: I mean ever.

B: You mean a discovery or mechanical thing. (See note at the end of 7A, page 82.)

A: It doesn't make any difference - just the most incredible thing.

B: Mm. I guess I'd have to say anesthetic.

A: Anesthetic?

B: Mm

A: Yeah. I guess anesthetic has made a very big impact.

B: So you agree?

A: Yes, I agree.

7B Exercise 1: b<u>l</u>ed   s<u>t</u>ep   <u>c</u>lean   <u>pl</u>ease   s<u>p</u>ell   <u>dr</u>ip   s<u>l</u>ip

    Exercise 2: fis<u>t</u>   lim<u>p</u>   wen<u>t</u>   lin<u>k</u>   sen<u>d</u>   sin<u>g</u>   buil<u>t</u>

7C

si~~g~~n   lim~~b~~s   r~~h~~ythm   ~~k~~nee   ans~~w~~er   ta~~l~~k   i~~s~~land   pa~~l~~m   ~~w~~rong

7D

1) a) Did you find the pen?

2) b) He put the bill on the table.

3) b) She's become a bitter person.

4) a) They found the medal.

5) a) The farmer built ten shelters for his animals in winter.

6) a) Could you press the left button for me, please?

7) b) I need a disk for my computer.

7E

1) a) Did you <u>find</u> the pen ?

2) b) He <u>put</u> the <u>bill</u> on the table .

3) b) She's become a bitter <u>person</u>.

4) a) They <u>found</u> the medal .

5) a) The <u>farmer</u> <u>built</u> ten <u>shelters</u> for his <u>animals</u> in winter .

6) a) Could you <u>press</u> the left button for me, <u>please</u>?

7) b) I <u>need</u> a disk for my com<u>pu</u>ter.

Part 8B

1) b) Did you collect the letter?

2) b) The limbs look strong.

3) a) Show me your wrist.

4) a) You're going the wrong way.

1B 1) b) I bought a belt.   2) b) I want to buy a card.
   3) b) Do you have the right time?   4) a) What day is it?

1C

/æ/ bat	/ɪ/ bit	/e/ bet	/ʌ/ but
j<u>a</u>m	g<u>y</u>m	g<u>e</u>m	m<u>o</u>ney
s<u>a</u>d	b<u>ui</u>lt	s<u>ai</u>d	l<u>u</u>mp
l<u>a</u>mp	l<u>i</u>mp	b<u>e</u>lt	w<u>o</u>n
	w<u>i</u>n	m<u>a</u>ny	r<u>u</u>st
	wr<u>i</u>st	wh<u>e</u>n	
		r<u>e</u>st	

1D

1)   b) The child has a limp.   2) a) Did they pack everything?
3)   d) There was a problem with the truck.   4) c) It's better.

Part 1 Introduction to the topic
b) There is a festival happening somewhere in the world almost every day of the year.

1B
1) saluted, greeted, praised _hailed_
2) things that happen _events_
3) holy people _saints_
4) nations/people of similar appearance and features _races_
5) of a long time ago _ancient_
6) happening _taking place_
7) public celebration _festival_
8) self-government, not controlled by another _independence_

Part 2A

1) Sound /e/ as in the word _pen_	2) Sound /eɪ/ as in the word _pain_
sp**e**cial c**e**lebrate	**a**ncient s**ai**nt
ev**e**nts	h**ai**led celebr**a**tion
h**e**ld	d**ay**s
c**e**ntury	r**a**ces
independ**e**nce	gr**ea**t
s**e**nt	pl**a**ce

2B

words with one syllable	words with two syllables	words with three syllables	words with four syllables
h**e**ld s**e**nt h**ai**led s**ai**nt d**ay**s gr**ea**t pl**a**ce	/ə/ sp**e**cial /ə/ ev**e**nts /ə/ **a**ncient /ə/ r**a**ces	/ə/ c**e**ntury /ə/ c**e**lebrate	/ə/ /ə/ independence /ə/ /ə/ celebration

Part 3B
1) make more attractive/beautiful _decorate_
2) amused/pleased _entertained_
3) activities played for fun _games_
4) to request or thank God _pray_
5) periods of time in the development of something _phases_
6) historical stories (which may not be true) _legends_
7) clothing _dress_
8) interesting stories _tales_
9) established on _based on_
10) calculate _measure_
11) a lot of _many_
12) public processions _parades_

Part 4

1) Words with the sound /e/ (as in _pen_)	2) Words with the sound /&/ (as in _pain_)
d**e**corate	enter**tai**ned b**a**sed (on)
l**e**gends	g**a**mes par**a**des
dr**e**ss	pr**ay**
m**e**asure	ph**a**ses
m**a**ny	tales

Part 7A
1) _What's your most_ popular cultural celebration?

2) _When do you_ celebrate it?

3) _How do you_ celebrate it?

4) _What's the main reason for_ celebrating it?

Unit 9 – Festival and Celebrations – Answers

7B
/ə/
1) <u>What</u>'s your <u>most</u> popular <u>cu</u>ltural cele<u>bra</u>tion?

/ə/ /ə/   /ə/
2) When do you <u>cele</u>brate it?

/ə//ə/   /ə/
3) How do you <u>cele</u>brate it?

/ə/   /ə/   /ə/
4) <u>What's</u> the <u>main</u> reason for <u>ce</u>lebrating it?

7C

verb	noun
eg. <u>cele</u>brate	cele<u>bra</u>tion
<u>e</u>ducate	edu<u>ca</u>tion
ex<u>a</u>mine	exami<u>na</u>tion
com<u>mu</u>nicate	communi<u>ca</u>tion

7D & 7E

1) *Ja<u>pan</u>*	*Japa<u>nese</u>*	5) *China*	*Chi<u>nese</u>*
2) *Egypt*	*E<u>gyp</u>tian*	6) *Portugal*	*Portu<u>guese</u>*
3) *<u>I</u>taly*	*I<u>ta</u>lian*	7) *Tonga*	*<u>Ton</u>gan*
4) *Canada*	*Ca<u>na</u>dian*		

7F

1) b) It's better not to make the children wait.

2) b) Where's the pain?

3) a) Where did you sell the boat?

4) b) Did he tell you about the date?

5) a) They saw the well near the rocks.

6) b) He tasted each variety of wine.

7) b) It's too hot here. Let's stand in the shade.

8) a) Could you put some pepper on the table please? (pepper = spice added to food)

7G

1) b) It's <u>better</u> not to make the <u>children</u> <u>wait</u>.

2) b) <u>Where</u>'s the pain ?

3) a) <u>Where</u> did you <u>sell</u> the boat ?

4) b) Did he <u>tell</u> <u>you</u> about the date ?

5) a) They <u>saw</u> the well near the rocks .

6) b) He <u>tasted</u> <u>each</u> <u>variety</u> of <u>wine</u>.   Note: In sentence 6) the speaker puts equal stress on each content word in the utterance, therefore no word is made more prominent than the others.

7) b) It's too hot here . Let's <u>stand</u> in the shade .

8) a) Could you <u>put</u> some pepper on the table <u>please</u>? (pepper = spice added to food)

Part 8C

1) a) They had a few of the games at their house.

2) b) The van isn't working properly.

3) a) The ocean liner is fast and comfortable for passengers.

4) b) The vines are much higher than last year.

Part 1 Introduction to the topic b) It's impossible to deny that life has changed in many ways.

1B

1) speed/rate of progress	*pace*	7) instantly, immediately	*instantaneously*
2) tell, talk about	*relate*	8) surprisingly	*amazingly*
3) type, kind of	*style*	9) walk a long way	*hike*
4) obtained/found/achieved	*gained*	10) say it is not true	*deny*
5) happened, occurred	*taken place*	11) bad, illegal action	*crime*
6) electronic mail	*e-mail*		

Part 2A

1) Sound /aɪ/ as in the word 'why'	2) Sound /eɪ/ as in the word 'way'
right　*hike* *life*　*deny* *style* *time* *crime*	*say*　*gained* *pace*　*sail* *same* *place* *mail*

2B

1) How's communication changed in the last twenty-five years?

2) How's transportation changed in the last twenty-five years?

3) How's education changed in the last twenty-five years?

4) How's entertainment changed in the last twenty-five years?

5) What changes've taken place in your life the last five years?

6) How do you think science'll change our lives in the next five years?

Part 3B

1) advanced technology	*high tech*	7) mechanical things	*devices*
2) accept, welcome	*embrace*	8) worrying, alarming	*frightening*
3) most recent	*latest*	9) regardless of	*despite*
4) suggestion	*advice*	10) not happy to wait	*impatient*
5) makes me angry/upset	*drives me crazy*	11) make a sound which	
6) sensible	*wise*	expresses unhappiness	*sigh*

Part 4A

Words with the sound /aɪ/ (as in *why*)	Words with the sound /eɪ/ (as in *way*)
drives　*devices* *style*　*despite* *I'm*　*advice* *wise*　*sigh*	*embrace*　*ways* *latest*　*say* *crazy* *sale* *aim*
4B　*satellite* 　　*microscope* 　　*microphone*	*plane*　*crane* *train* *x-ray*

Part 5B

kit	kite	hat	hate
hid	hide	cap	cape
pin	pine	rat	rate
bit	bite	tap	tape
quit	quite	mat	mate

Part 7A

Mike: *Life's changed* since I was a child. *I don't like the* pace of life these days.

Kay: Why do you say that? *I think life's* great these days.

Mike: *I feel like I'm* racing with time. *There're too many* changes.

Kay: But *if times didn't* change, *life wouldn't be* very exciting!

Mike: Mm. *You're* probably right. But it drives me crazy just the same.

7C

1) b) Where's the pain?

2) a) I'm going to have a light lunch today. (light lunch = small lunch)

3) b) Did he finish his race?

4) b) The plane's later than last time.

5) b) Could you tape the lecture for me, please? (tape = record)

6) a) It's important to give the right prize to the winner. (prize = reward)

7) a) I'm to finish the report by Friday.

7D

1) b) Where's the pain?

2) a) I'm going to have a light lunch today. (light lunch = small lunch)

3) b) Did he finish his race?

4) b) The plane's later than last time.

5) b) Could you tape the lecture for me, please? (tape = record)

6) a) It's important to give the right prize to the winner. (prize = reward)

7) a) I'm to finish the report by Friday.

Part 8A

1) /g/ as in the word 'game'	2) silent /g/	3) /dʒ / as in the word 'page'
gained	sigh	change
begin	weight	manage
great	high	gem
regular		
game		

Title Page: The sports illustrated are horse riding, surfing, soccer, volleyball, golf, hockey, cricket, tennis.

Part 1 Introduction to the topic

a) Most reporters suggest that sport generally has <u>positive</u> effect on people.

1B

1) in summary, briefly	_(in) a word_	6) strict/definite	_firm_
2) an area for playing games	_court_	7) to make/ build	_form_
3) compelled, with no choice	_forced_	8) type/variety	_sort_
4) points won in a game	_scores_	9) do/act	_perform_
5) people who watch or listen	_audience(s)_	10) prize or payment	_award_
		11) past form of 'fight'	_fought_

Part 2A

1) Sound /ɜ:/ as in the word '*work*'	2) Sound /ɔ:/ as in the word '*walk*'
_fi<u>r</u>m_ _lea<u>r</u>n_ _fi<u>r</u>st_ _a w<u>or</u>d_ _w<u>or</u>k_	_f<u>or</u>m_ _audiences_ _c<u>our</u>t_ _sc<u>or</u>es_ _s<u>or</u>t_ _f<u>ough</u>t_ _f<u>or</u>ced_ _aw<u>ar</u>d_

2C

1) Words ending /əz/ or /ɪz/	2) Words ending /z/	3) Words ending /s/
mi<u>ss</u>es fini<u>sh</u>es do<u>z</u>es wa<u>tch</u>es ju<u>dg</u>es ra<u>c</u>es ca<u>tch</u>es	w<u>ar</u>s /w ɔːz/ follows all vowel sounds ba<u>ll</u>s ba<u>g</u>s ser<u>v</u>es ga<u>m</u>es ru<u>l</u>es stars /staːz/	ma<u>k</u>es ge<u>t</u>s ma<u>p</u>s lau<u>gh</u>s /laːfs/ loo<u>k</u>s ba<u>t</u>s
The sound /əz/ follows sounds: /s/ /ʃ/ /z/ /s/ /tʃ/ /dʒ/	The sound /z/ follows vowel sounds and sounds /b/ /d/ /g/ /l/ /m/ /n/ /r/ /v/	The sound /s/ follows sounds: /k/ /t/ /p/ /f/

Part 3B

1) fair, honest competition	_sportsmanship_	5) good, respectable	_worthy_
2) excellence/greatness	_glory_	6) aim, intended result	_purpose_
3) promote, advance	_further_	7) definitely	_certainly_
4) help, assist	_serve_	8) arranged	_organised_

Part 4

Words with the sound /ɜ:/ as in *work*	Words with the sound /ɔ:/ as in *walk*
f<u>ur</u>ther _s<u>er</u>ve_ _w<u>or</u>thy_ _p<u>ur</u>pose_ _c<u>er</u>tainly_	_sportsmanship_ _gl<u>ory</u>_ _<u>or</u>ganised_

Part 6 Check your answers by comparing what you've written with the text in Part 1A.

7B Do you pre<u>fer</u> playing or watching sport?   Note: The contrasting words are made most prominent.

Do you pre<u>fer</u> indoor or outdoor sport?

Do you pre<u>fer</u> individual or team sport?

7D

A: Look what I've just bought at the *sports* store, some *shorts*, some *shirts*, four soccer balls, a drawing board, some golf *balls*, and some assorted ball games.

B: It looks like you've bought the whole *store*.

A: I know, but there's *more*. I've also ordered *four* surfboards.

B: Four surfboards? What on earth for?

A: For birthday presents for Paul and Dawn and my *daughters*. All their birthdays are in *August*, so it's perfect. And everything in the store was forty percent off the normal price.

B: *Forty* percent? That's a bargain. I should call into the store after *work*.

A: I think it closes at *four thirty* and the sale finishes tomorrow morning. Why don't you give them a *call*?

B: OK. Do you know the number?

A: Yes I have it here. It's *324 729 454*.

B: *324 729 454*. I'll call them now. I could use a new *surfboard* and some new shirts.

7D   **Pausing and intonation - answers**

A: Look what I've just bought at the sports store/ some shorts/ some shirts/ four soccer balls/ a drawing board/ some golf balls/ and some assorted ball games/.

B: It looks like you've bought the whole store.

A: I know, but there's more. I've also ordered four surfboards.

B: Four surfboards? What on earth for?

A: For birthday presents for Paul and Dawn and my daughters. All their birthdays are in August, so it's perfect. And everything in the store was forty percent off the normal price.

B: Forty percent? That's a bargain. I should call into the store after work.

A: I think it closes at four thirty and the sale finishes tomorrow morning. Why don't you give them a call?

B: OK. Do you know the number?

A: Yes I have it here. It's 324 /729/ 454/.

B: 324 /729/ 454/. I'll call them now. I could use a new surfboard and some new shirts.

7E   1) b) I walked for a long time today.

2) b) He was forced to say he was wrong.

3) a) You bought a new bird yesterday?

4) a) How much are the blue shirts?

5) a) I need to check a word in the dictionary.

6) b) I'm going to walk in the park tomorrow.

7) b) I asked a lot of questions about the form.   ('form' = 'written report')

7F

1) b) I <u>walked</u> for a long time today.

2) b) He was forced to <u>say</u> he was wrong.

3) a) You bought a <u>new</u> bird yesterday?

(Rising intonation here implies surprise and uncertainty. (meaning '*But I thought you already had a bird.*')

4) a) How <u>much</u> are the blue shirts?

5) a) I <u>need</u> to <u>check</u> a <u>word</u> in the dictionary.

6) b) I'm <u>going</u> to <u>walk</u> in the park tomorrow.

7) b) I <u>asked</u> a <u>lot</u> of <u>questions</u> about the form.

Review – Long vowel sounds

1A

/ɑː/ as in *far*	/ɜː/ as in *fur*	/ɔː/ as in *four*
farm	*firm*	*form*
a card	*occurred*	*accord*
star	*stir*	*store*
heart	*hurt*	*born*
barn	*burn*	

1B   1) c) What did you think of the form?   2) a) Did you see the bar?

3) b) He was first to do it.   4) a) It's a card.

Part 1 Introduction to the topic a) People need a plan in order to achieve their goal.
1B

1) a choice	*option*	5) the target, aim	*goal*
2) not weak	*strong*	6) clearly see/give attention to	*focus*
3) a series of lessons	*course*	7) great interest in doing (something)	*motivation*
4) develop	*evolve*	8) information repeated or copied from another person	*quote*

1C 1) An option is a choice between more than one possible way or decision.
　　2) A goal is the object of a person's future plan.
　　3) Reaching a goal involves a plan; focussing on the goal and having strong motivation.

Part 2A

1) vowel sound in the word c*o*t	2) vowel sound in the word c*ou*rt	3) vowel sound in the word c*oa*t
*o*ption	m*o*re	g*oa*l　　　　sh*ow*s
j*o*b	c*ou*rse	f*o*cus
str*o*ng	*a*lw*a*ys	kn*ow*
ev*o*lve	t*a*lk	qu*o*te

2B　　　　　If you think you can / or if you think you can't / you're probably right.

Part 3A Note: This is not the only correct way of reading this text. A different reader may pause in different
　　　　　places depending on what information s/he feels goes together in the text.
　　　　　Note: You may notice additional *very short pauses* which have not been marked here.

What's the difference between an option /and a goal?/ An option/ is a choice between
more than one possible way or decision./ A goal on the other hand, /is the object of a
person's future plan./ It's what a person wants and hopes for in the future./ Most people
hope for good things in the future/ but not everyone has a goal./ Reaching a goal involves
more than just talking about what we want./ It involves a plan of action./ It also involves
focussing on the goal /and having strong motivation./

A lot of people are not sure about their goals./ They may know they want to do a university course/ get a
better job/ go overseas/ or one day own a home of their own/ but they don't really have a plan/ they just hope
that one day it'll happen./ But hopes don't always evolve/ unless we plan for them/ and then focus on the
goal./

Confidence in your own ability to reach your goal is also important /as the following
quote by Henry Ford shows/

　　　　　'If you think you can/ or if you think you can't/ you're probably right.'

/The process of reaching your goal involves several important steps./

1/ Decide *what* you want or hope for/ by writing a list of the pros and cons of all your
　options./When you've reached a decision,/write down your goal./

2/ Decide *when* you want to achieve your goal. /Be practical about this./
　Ask yourself: /What's possible? /What's not possible?/

3/ Give thought to the steps you'll need to take to reach your goal./
　What knowledge are you going to need to achieve your goal? /
　What obstacles and problems will you need to overcome? /
　Generally problems won't stop you reaching your goal if you stay focussed./
　In fact overcoming problems can often make your resolve stronger.

4/ Divide your long term goal into several short term goals./
　Then focus on your short term goals./

5/ Be positive about your progress./ Don't only look at how far you need to go;/
　also look at how far you've already progressed along the road toward your goal!/

3B

1) advantages and disadvantages
   of an action or decision — *pros and cons*
2) confident, definite — *positive*
3) the path/way of going — *road*
4) method of doing something — *process*
5) may be achieved — *possible*
6) information gained by
   learning — *knowledge*
7) will not — *won't*
8) problems — *obstacles*
9) a strong mental decision — *resolve*
10) relating to a long
    period of time — *long (term)*

Part 4

Words with the vowel sound as in *cot*		Words with the vowel sound as in *coat*
(pros and) cons	*obstacles*	*pros (and cons)*
positive	*resolve*	*road*
possible	*long*	*process*
knowledge		*won't*

Part 7A

Joan: You know how I've been talking about going overseas?/

Bob: You're always talking about it./

Joan: Well, I've decided to make a goal to go in November./

Bob: November? / It's already August. /That's only four months off./ How will you afford it?/

Joan: Well I've set myself some goals. /I'm going to quit smoking, /make a lot less phone calls,/ walk more instead of using public transport./ And I'm going to do more overtime at work/. By October I should have enough money to go./

Bob: Quit smoking? /Walk more? /Are you joking? /I've heard all this before./

Joan: I know / but this time I feel very motivated./ So /If I can stay focussed on the goal I know I'll be in Rome by the end of November. / Mm ... I'll have to start thinking about clothes./ Is it hot or cold in Rome in November?/

Bob: Mm. I'm not sure./ It'll be cold I think./

7A Revision exercises - Linking and intonation

Joan: You know how⌣I've been talking⌣about going⌣overseas?/

Bob: You'r(e)⌣always talking⌣about it./

Joan: Well, I've decided to make⌣a goal to go⌣in⌣November./

Bob: November? /It's⌣already⌣August. /That's⌣only four months⌣off./ How⌣will you⌣afford⌣it?/ /w/ (over November) /w/ (over you)

Joan: Well, I've set myself some goals. /I'm going to quit smoking, /mak(e)⌣a lot less phone calls,/ walk more instead of using public transport./ And I'm going to do more overtime at work./ By⌣October⌣I should hav(e)⌣enough money to go./

Bob: Quit smoking? /Walk more? /Are you joking? /I've heard⌣all this before./

Joan: I know / but this time⌣I feel very motivated./ So /If⌣I can stay focussed⌣on the goal⌣I know⌣I'll be⌣in Rome by the⌣end⌣of November. / Mm ... I'll have to start thinking⌣about clothes./ Is⌣it hot⌣or cold⌣in Rom(e)⌣in⌣November?/ /j/ /j/

Bob: Mm. I'm not sure./ It'll be cold⌣I think./

7B

eg. W<u>a</u>shington *city*   Se<u>ou</u>l *city*   Sc<u>o</u>tland *country (part of the United Kingdom)*

R<u>o</u>me *city*   P<u>o</u>land *country*   Osl<u>o</u> *city*   Cair<u>o</u> *city*

Quit<u>o</u> *city*   Mong<u>o</u>lia *city*   Toky<u>o</u> *city*   Cong<u>o</u> *country*

7C

Places with the vowel sound (as in *cot*)	Places with the vowel sound (as in *coat*)	
W<u>a</u>shington Sc<u>o</u>tland	Se<u>ou</u>l R<u>o</u>me P<u>o</u>land Osl<u>o</u>	Cair<u>o</u> Quit<u>o</u> Mong<u>o</u>lia Toky<u>o</u> Cong<u>o</u>

7D

Hot/Warm – November to March	Cold – November to March	
Cong<u>o</u> Quit<u>o</u>	W<u>a</u>shington Sc<u>o</u>tland Se<u>ou</u>l R<u>o</u>me P<u>o</u>land	Cair<u>o</u> Mong<u>o</u>lia Toky<u>o</u> Osl<u>o</u>

7E
1) b) I'd like to buy a <u>coat</u>, please.
2) a) I can't find the right <u>rod</u>.
3) a) He told me about the <u>cost</u>.
4) b) She <u>hopes</u> every day to get slimmer.
5) b) How do you spell '<u>robe</u>'?
6) a) Can you help me with this <u>knot</u>?
7) b) The students <u>won't</u> tell.
8) a) They <u>want</u> work.

7F
1) b) I'd <u>like</u> to <u>buy</u> a coat, please.
2) a) I <u>can't</u> <u>find</u> the <u>right</u> rod
3) a) He <u>told</u> me about the cost.
4) b) She hopes every <u>day</u> to get <u>slimmer</u>.
5) b) <u>How</u> do you <u>spell</u> 'robe'?
6) a) Can you <u>help</u> me with this knot?
7) b) The <u>students</u> <u>won't</u> tell.
8) a) They <u>want</u> work.

(Note: This is the same test as in Unit 1 – Part 3 - Listening Test – Check your progress!)

Listening Test - Exercise 1

1) b) They're <u>leaving</u> on a boat.
2) b) I left my <u>cup</u> in the kitchen.
3) a) Have they <u>packed</u> the car yet?
4) a) How do you spell '<u>full</u>'?
5) b) I need a <u>disk</u> for my computer.
6) a) Did you see the little boy's <u>mouth</u>?

7) b) How many <u>bears</u> did you see?
8) b) Where's the <u>pain</u>?
9) a) I <u>worked</u> for a long time today.
10) a) Did he finish his <u>rice</u>?
11) a) They <u>want</u> work.
12) b) They went the <u>wrong</u> way.
13) a) The <u>men</u> listened to the story.

Listening Test - Exercise 2

1) a) <u>pre</u>sent
2) b) ob<u>ject</u>

3) a) <u>de</u>sert
4) b) pro<u>duce</u>

Listening Test - Exercise 3

A: Could you <u>tell</u> me where the <u>bank</u> is <u>please</u>?

B: <u>Yes,</u> in <u>High</u> Street, on the <u>left</u>, near the <u>library</u>.

A: <u>Thanks</u>. And is there <u>some</u>where to <u>park</u> the <u>car</u>?

B: There's a <u>place</u> just <u>next</u> to the <u>bank</u> but you'll have to <u>pay</u>.

A: Oh. Do you <u>know</u> what they <u>charge</u>?

B: I <u>don't,</u> I'm <u>sorry</u> - but there'll be a <u>sign</u> at the <u>gate</u> with the <u>price</u>.

There's also a <u>place</u> near the <u>station</u>. It's usually <u>full</u> but you could <u>check</u>.

A: OK. <u>Thanks</u> for your <u>help</u>.

Listening Test – Exercise 4

In sentences with contractions, both the contracted form and the full form have been given below. Either answer can be counted as correct – though notice that the speakers on the audio recording use contractions. For information about contractions, see Unit 2, Part 8A.

1) What's your phone number?
   (What is your phone number?)   (five words)

2) How do you spell your surname?   (six words)

3) I'll check on the computer.
   (I will check on the computer.)   (six words)

4) I can send some information if you're interested.
   (I can send some information if you are interested.)   (nine words)

5) I'd like to speak to someone now if possible.
   (I would like to speak to someone now if possible.)   (ten words)

Phonemic Chart of English Sounds

(Below each sound symbol are examples of words containing the sound.)

Vowel sounds

æ (short sound)	e (short sound)	ɒ (short sound)	ə (unstressed sound)
bl**a**ck	r**e**d	…. d**o**ts ….	oth**er** broth**er**
ɑː (long sound)	ʊ (short sound)	ʌ (short sound)	ɪ (short sound)
c**ar**	g**oo**d	f**u**n	p**i**nk
ɜː (long sound)	uː (long sound)	ɔː (long sound)	iː (long sound)
p**ur**ple	bl**ue**	f**ou**r m**ore**	gr**ee**n

Diphthong (two vowel) sounds

eɪ	ɔɪ	əʊ (also oʊ)	ɪə
gr**ey**	b**oy**	yell**ow** g**o**ld	cl**ear** b**eer**
eə (also ɛə)	aɪ	ʊə	aʊ
h**air**	br**igh**t l**i**me	t**our**	br**ow**n m**ou**se

Consonant sounds

Note: voiceless sounds are shown in a shaded box. See page 32 for an explanation.

p	b	t	d
pet **p**ig	**b**ig **b**ag	**t**ell **t**wo	**d**irty **d**og
tʃ	dʒ	k	g
Chinese **ch**ild	**j**ust **j**oking	**k**eep **c**ool	**g**ood **g**irl
f	v	θ	ð
fill **f**our	**v**ery **v**ivid	**th**ink **th**in	o**th**er bro**th**er
s	z	ʃ	ʒ
sad **s**ong	**z**ig-**z**ag	**sh**ort **sh**eep	mea**s**ure A**si**a
m	n	ŋ	h
milk **m**an	**n**o **n**ever	lo**ng** so**ng**	**h**ot **h**ill
l	r	w	j
little **l**ine	**r**ice	**w**et **w**inter	**y**es **y**ou

As the pronunciation of some English vowel sounds varies across and within countries, the examples given on this chart are intended as a general guide

Boyer Educational Resources books and audio

'Understanding Spoken English' – (books and audio) international editions

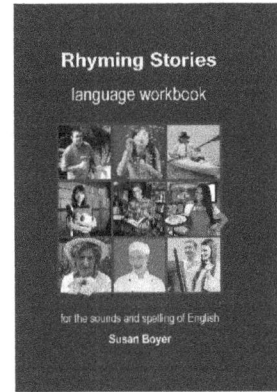

Understanding Spoken English — Book One — a focus on everyday language in context — Contains: dialogues, language reviews, answers and reference lists — Susan Boyer — Use with accompanying audio recording

Understanding Spoken English — Book Two — a focus on everyday language in context — Contains: dialogues, language reviews, answers and reference lists — Susan Boyer — Use with accompanying audio recording

Understanding Spoken English — Book Three — a focus on everyday language in context — Susan Boyer — international edition

Rhyming Stories — language workbook — for the sounds and spelling of English — Susan Boyer

'Understanding Everyday Australian' – series (books and audio)

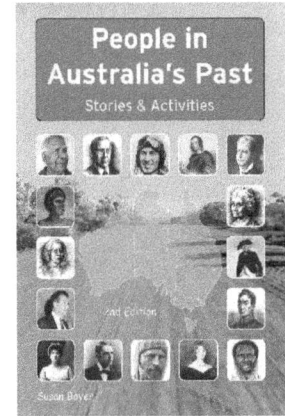

Book One — UNDERSTANDING Everyday Australian — A focus on spoken language with language reviews, exercises and answers. — To be used with audio cassette. — by Susan Boyer

Book Two — UNDERSTANDING Everyday Australian — A focus on spoken language with language reviews, exercises and answers. — To be used with audio cassette. — by Susan Boyer

Book Three — UNDERSTANDING Everyday Australian — A focus on spoken language with language reviews, exercises and answers — To be used with audio recording — Susan Boyer

People in Australia's Past — Stories & Activities — 2nd Edition — Susan Boyer

| Spelling and Pronunciation for English Language Learners | Understanding English Pronunciation | Word Building Activities for beginners of English | English Language Skills Level One |

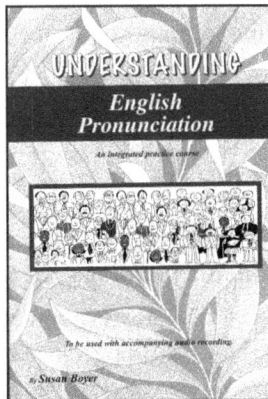

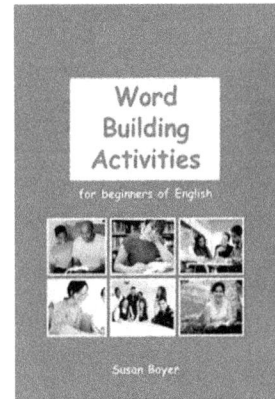

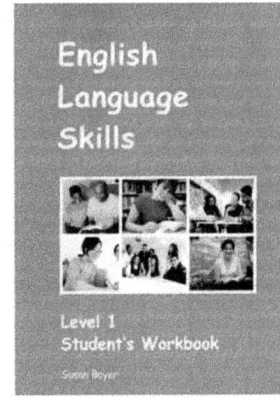

SPELL — Spelling and Pronunciation for English Language Learners — Susan Boyer — Practice Book

UNDERSTANDING English Pronunciation — An integrated practice course — To be used with accompanying audio recording — by Susan Boyer

Word Building Activities — for beginners of English — Susan Boyer

English Language Skills — Level 1 Student's Workbook — Susan Boyer

Teacher's Books with photocopiable activities such as surveys, role-cards & vocabulary activities

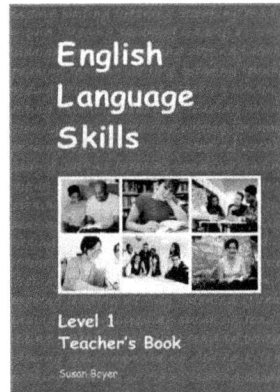

Book Two — UNDERSTANDING Everyday Australian — A focus on spoken language with communicative activities to enhance learning and promote classroom interaction. — by Susan Boyer — Teacher's Book

UNDERSTANDING English Pronunciation — An integrated practice course — Teacher's Book — by Susan Boyer

Understanding Spoken English — Teacher's Book Three — Teacher's photocopiable activities for classroom interaction — Susan Boyer — international edition

English Language Skills — Level 1 Teacher's Book — Susan Boyer

All teacher's books are A4 size. Student's books contain language exercises and answers.

All resources are available as either PDF or MP3 downloads via www.boyereducation.com.au

ACROSS GREAT DIVIDES

true stories of life at Sydney Cove

SUSAN E BOYER

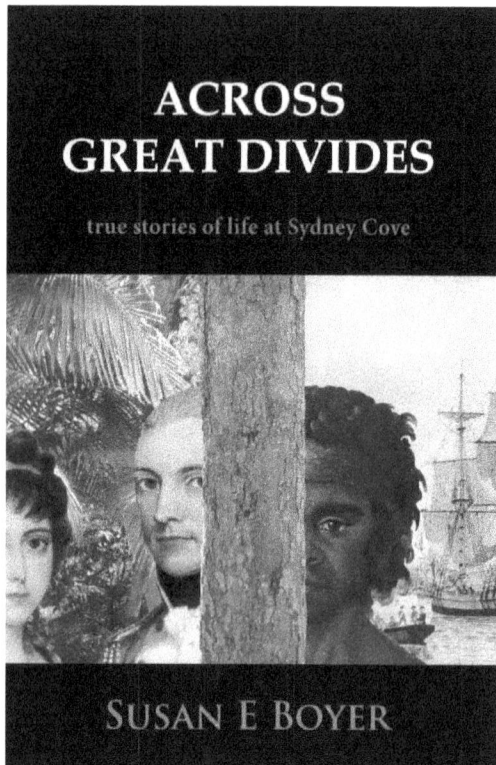

'Across Great Divides: True Stories of Life at Sydney Cove' is a non-fiction narrative that brings to life the experiences of convicts, marines and officers aboard the First Fleet and after their arrival in Sydney Cove. These true stories show the varied responses to their unique situation in Australia's first colony. The stories cover the period from 1787 to 1792.

The stories also give voice to the dilemma of the Aboriginal people challenged by the unexpected arrival of a completely alien race of white people to their land. Yet meetings between the cultures were dynamic and varied.

The mystery of a new world had begun and the lives of all involved would never be the same again.

> **'Across Great Divides –**
> true stories of life at Sydney Cove'
> ISBN: 978 1 8770744 2 4
> **Available from online bookstores and**
> **online from Birrong Books at www.birrongbooks.com**
> **ePub version available from ePub platforms**

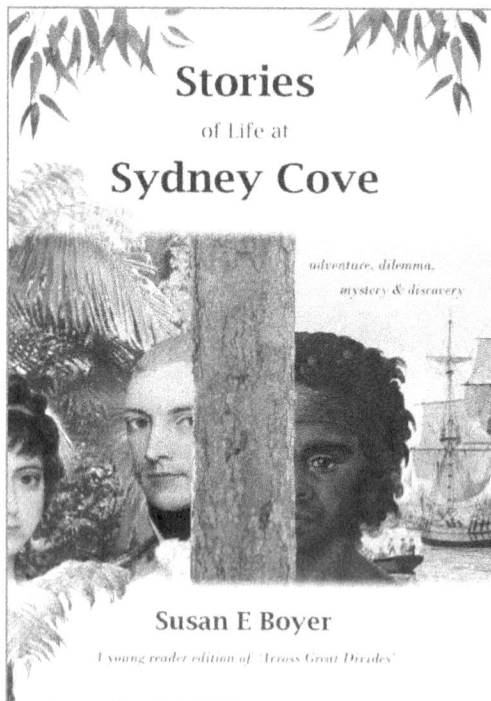

Stories of Life at Sydney Cove

adventure, dilemma, mystery & discovery

Susan E Boyer

A young reader edition of 'Across Great Divides'

'Stories of Life at Sydney Cove', follows the success of 'Across Great Divides'. It is written for younger readers as historical fiction, but the stories are about real people.

****

When thirteen-year-old convicts, John and Elizabeth, are sent to a mysterious land at the end of the world, they have no idea what life holds for them. At Sydney Cove there are no roads, no fences, no buildings... just wilderness.

Later when Indigenous children Nanberry and Boorong come to live with the white strangers, they see life through different eyes.

> **'Stories of Life at Sydney Cove'**
> ISBN: 978 1 877074 4 9 3
>
> **Available from online bookstores and**
> **online from Birrong Books at www.birrongbooks.com**
>
> See links to Australian History and English Curriculum below and find free teaching and learning resources at
> www.birrongbooks.com

Information below sourced from **Australian Curriculum** – History Units Content:
Ver 8.4 (Yrs 3-6) and Ver 9.0 (Yrs 7-10)

Year 4 - Learning area content descriptions
Stories of the First Fleet, including reasons for the journey, who travelled to Australia, and their experiences following arrival. (ACHASSK085)
The nature of contact between Aboriginal and Torres Strait Islander Peoples. (ACHASSK086)
Year 5 - Learning area content descriptions
The nature of convict or colonial presence, including the factors that influenced patterns of development, aspects of the daily life of the inhabitants and how the environment changed. (ACHASSK107)
Year 9 - Making and transforming the Australian nation (1750–1914)
The causes and effects of European contact and extension of settlement, including their impact on the First Nations Peoples of Australia. (AC9HH9K03)

Boyer Educational Resources

e-mail: info@boyereducation.com.au
websites: www.boyereducation.com.au   www.englishebooks.com

Title	ISBN
Across Great Divides - true stories of life at Sydney Cove	**978 1 877074 42 4**
Stories of Life at Sydney Cove	**978 1 877074 49 3**
People in Australia's Past - Stories & Activities (2nd Edition, A4)	978 1 877074 46 2
People in Australia's Past - Audio CD (2nd Edition)	978 1 877074 47 9
People in Australia's Past - Stories & Activities Book with CD (2nd ED)	**978 1 877074 48 6**
Understanding Everyday Australian - Book One	978 0 958539 50 0
Understanding Everyday Australian - Audio CD One (1)	978 1 877074 01 1
Understanding Everyday Australian - Teacher's Book One	978 0 958539 52 4
Understanding Everyday Australian - Book One & Audio CD	**978 1 877074 16 5**
Understanding Everyday Australian - Book Two	978 0 958539 53 1
Understanding Everyday Australian - Audio CD Two (1)	978 1 877074 02 8
Understanding Everyday Australian - Teacher's Book Two	978 0 958539 55 5
Understanding Everyday Australian - Book Two & Audio CD	**978 1 877074 17 2**
Understanding Everyday Australian - Book Three	978 1 877074 20 2
Understanding Everyday Australian - Audio CD Three	978 1 877074 21 9
Understanding Everyday Australian - Teacher's Book Three	978 1 877074 22 6
Understanding Everyday Australian - Book Three & Audio CD	**978 1 877074 23 3**
Word Building Activities for Beginners of English	978 1 877074 28 8
English Language Skills - Level One Student's Workbook	978 1 877074 29 5
English Language Skills - Level One Audio CD	978 1 877074 31 8
English Language Skills - Level One Teacher's Book	978 1 877074 32 5
English Language Skills - Level 1 Teacher's Book & Audio CD	**987 1 877074 33 2**
Rhyming Stories - practice with the sounds and spelling of English (A5)	978 1 877074 06 6
Rhyming Stories -audio CD	978 1 877074 37 0
Rhyming Stories - language workbook (A4)	978 1 877074 38 7
English Vowel Sound Spelling Charts - A4 colour laminated & reusable	978 1 877074 39 4
Phonemic Charts - 2 x A3 Laminated - Vowel and Consonant	978 1 877074 05 9
Spelling and Pronunciation for English Language Learners	978 1 877074 04 2
Understanding English Pronunciation - Student book only	978 0 958539 57 9
Understanding English Pronunciation - Audio CD (Set of 3)	978 1 877074 03 5
Understanding English Pronunciation - Teacher's Book	**978 0 958539 59 3**
Understanding Spoken English - Book One	978 1 877074 08 0
Understanding Spoken English - Audio CD One (1)	978 1 877074 10 3
Understanding Spoken English - Teacher's Book One	978 1 877074 11 0
Understanding Spoken English - Book One & Audio CD	**978 1 877074 18 9**
Understanding Spoken English - Book Two	978 1 877074 12 7
Understanding Spoken English - Audio CD Two (1)	978 1 877074 14 1
Understanding Spoken English - Teacher's Book Two	978 1 877074 15 8
Understanding Spoken English - Book Two & Audio CD	**978 1 877074 19 6**
Understanding Spoken English - Book Three	978 1 877074 24 0
Understanding Spoken English - Audio CD Three	978 1 877074 25 7
Understanding Spoken English - Teacher's Book Three	978 1 877074 26 4
Understanding Spoken English - Book Three & Audio CD	**978 1 877074 27 1**

Focus on Australian content

Beginner English

Pronunciation & Spelling

Focus on 'International English'

www.ingramcontent.com/pod-product-compliance
Lightning Source LLC
Chambersburg PA
CBHW081135090426
42742CB00016BA/2871